European
COMPUTER
Driving
LICENCE

Alan Clarke

Hodder & Stoughton
A MEMBER OF THE HODDER HEADLINE GROUP

Acknowledgements

To my wife and sons for their help and support during the writing of the book and particularly to Christine and Peter for their suggestions.

Orders: please contact Bookpoint Ltd, 78 Milton Park, Abingdon, Oxon OX14 4TD. Telephone: (44) 01235 827720, Fax: (44) 01235 400454. Lines are open from 9.00– 6.00, Monday to Saturday, with a 24 hour message answering service. Email address: orders@bookpoint.co.uk

British Library Cataloguing in Publication Data
A catalogue record for this title is available from The British Library

ISBN 0 340 782218

First published 2001
Impression number   10 9 8 7 6 5 4 3 2 1
Year   2005 2004 2003 2002 2001

Copyright © 2001 Alan Clarke

Typeset by Multiplex Techniques Ltd, Brook Industrial Park, Mill Brook Road, St. Mary Cray, Kent BR5 3SR.
Printed in Great Britain for Hodder & Stoughton Educational, a division of Hodder Headline Plc, 338 Euston Road, London NW1 3BH by J W Arrowsmith Ltd, Bristol.

Contents

Foreword

Information and Communication Technology (ICT) is changing the world in which we live, work and learn. This is not a new revolution but one which has been growing and accelerating since the first computer was designed. Initially, information technology was the preserve of a small group of scientists and technicians. However, this has steadily changed and now it is easy to see a time in the near future when everyone will need to be a competent user of information and communication technologies. New occupations have been created and others changed beyond recognition by ICT. Computers are an everyday object in most businesses, schools, doctors' surgeries, banks and building societies. Many families have bought computers to help their children's education, to take advantage of the opportunity to work from home or simply to discover what the World Wide Web has to offer.

Society has been so changed by Information and Communication Technology that many people believe a new type of society is developing which is based on access to information and knowledge. It is usually called the Information Society. For individuals, communities and organisations it is rapidly becoming essential to be ICT competent or risk being excluded from the emerging world of knowledge.

The European Computer Driving Licence (ECDL) is a standard which is accepted across Europe and North America. It shows that the holder is a competent user of ICT. The qualification is based on demonstrating your ability to use and understand the main computer and communication technology applications as well as showing your overall knowledge of computing.

This book aims to assist you with your studies to achieve ECDL. ECDL consists of seven modules. The first module aims to help you gain a theoretical understanding of computing. It provides much of the underpinning knowledge you need to become a competent computer user. The remaining six modules are intended to provide a solid practical base. Each practical module concentrates on a major application. The six modules cover:

- Using a computer
- Word-processing
- Spreadsheets
- Databases
- Presentation
- Information and Communication Technologies

There is a chapter devoted to each practical module while Chapters 1 and 2 concentrate on the theoretical content of the qualification. However, each practical chapter also contains details of how and in what context the application is used; therefore theoretical knowledge is spread throughout the book. It is provided when it is most appropriate.

Throughout the book there are many exercises and worked examples. The book is intended to allow you to apply the ideas and approaches to a range of versions of the applications (e.g. Microsoft Office 97 or 2000). Each chapter begins with a straightforward statement of what you will be able to do and understand by studying the chapter.

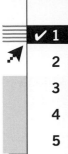

Basics of hardware and software

By the end of this chapter you should understand:

- the nature of the different types of computer;

- the component parts of a computer system;

- computer input and output devices;

- computer memory;

- application and operating system software;

- computer networks.

The chapter is divided into tutorials which include exercises that will allow you to practise many of the ideas presented in the text. Each exercise indicates how long it should take you to complete. They can be undertaken anywhere you can gain access to a computer – work, college, a local library or at home.

The tutorials in this chapter are as follows:

▶ TUTORIAL 1.1 What is a computer system?

A computer system consists of two main components:

- hardware

- software

Hardware comprises the physical aspects of the system. It consists of the parts that you can see and touch. There is a range of different pieces of hardware including monitors, storage devices (e.g. hard disk, CD-ROM and zip drives), keyboard, mouse and printer.

Software provides the instructions which make the hardware come to life. It takes two forms – the operating system and the application software. The operating system links the hardware and software together and provides many of the standard features of the computer. These include saving information on to the hard and floppy disks, printing documents, linking the keyboard and mouse to the application and presenting the information on the monitor. There are many different operating systems available to the computer user. This book is intended to be used in conjunction with the Microsoft Windows 98 operating system but is also suitable for Microsoft Windows 95 and 2000. Microsoft Windows is the most used Personal Computer (PC) operating system in the world. However, there are several other operating systems for PCs, such as Linux, MS-Dos and BeOS. Operating systems take on a variety of forms depending on the type of computer and the nature of the tasks which it needs to perform. They include:

Figure 1.1 Microsoft Windows 98 – Graphical User Interface

Figure 1.2 MS-DOS (Microsoft Disk Operating System)

MS-DOS – a single-tasking operating system which allows you to run a single program at any one time;

Windows 95 – a multitasking operating system which allows you to run more than one program at a time;

UNIX – a multiuser operating system that allows many users to use the computer system at the same time. It is also the basis of the Linux Operating System.

Each operating system employs a different style that users communicate with via the interface. Windows 95, 98 and 2000 employ a graphical user interface (GUI) (Figure 1.1) while MS-DOS uses a command line interface (Figure 1.2). A GUI is generally accepted as being easier for new, occasional or non-expert

users since many of the controls are visible on the screen. In contrast, a command line interface requires an experienced or expert user since you must remember a range of commands in order to make use of its functions. Other operating systems have attempted to combine the two approaches.

Application software allows specific tasks to be performed such as sending e-mail, keeping accounts, presenting information, collating information, manipulating photographs and writing documents. Each type of task requires a specific type of application software. In this book we will consider the applications provided by Microsoft Office 97 and 2000 which include word-processing, spreadsheets, databases, presentation and communication applications.

▶ Microsoft Windows

Duration 30 minutes

Exercise 1.1

1 Microsoft Windows is available in a range of versions including 95, 98 and 2000. It does not matter which version you have access to, but it is important that you become familiar with the nature of an operating system.

2 Operating systems load automatically when you switch on the computer and once Microsoft Windows is loaded you will see a display similar

to Figure 1.1. It will not be identical, since users of Microsoft Windows can customise and change the display to meet their needs. However, it should reveal something similar to Figure 1.3, that is, the desktop which occupies most of the screen, a button called Start in the bottom left-hand corner and a number of icons which link the display to various applications and features of the computer system.

Figure 1.3 Windows Desktop

Figure 1.4 Start Menu

3 Click on the Start button and a menu will appear (Figure 1.4). This shows you the basic functions that the operating system provides. Most have a small black triangle alongside. This indicates that if you place your mouse pointer on it, then other options will appear. The functions are:

- Shut Down – allows you to shut down the operating system in preparation for switching off the computer;

- Run – allows you to run programs, browse files and folders; Run is often used to install programs although there are other ways to perform this function;

- Help – provides access to the operating system's help function;

- Find – a very useful function which locates any file or folder on the system;

- Settings – provides access to many of the functions to set up and manage the computer system;

- Documents – lists the documents users have most recently used;

- Favourites – lists the users' list of favourite websites;

- Programs – provides access to the applications that are available on the computer system.

Explore each function to familarise yourself with the options and layout. In particular consider the Settings options (Figure 1.5) which allows you to manage the computer system settings (e.g. display resolutions, input and output devices, multimedia options and establishing passwords). Don't change anything but simply explore and observe. In the Control Panel see if you can identify the Display (this allows you to change the background colours of the system and screen saver options), Printers, System (this allows you to see what equipment is installed on your system and the system performance), Date/Time (allows you to change the computer systems date and time) and Add/Remove Programs. The latter allows you to install programs or remove them from your computer system. You access them by selecting (single click) the Control Panel option which reveals the display shown in Figure 1.6. During the exploration you will see examples of toolbars and scrollbars (Figure 1.6).

4 To close the function click on the small button with a cross in the top right-hand corner of the window. This will return you to the Desktop where the Start button resides.

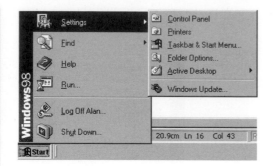

Figure 1.5 Settings

Figure 1.6 Control Panel

► TUTORIAL 1.2   Personal computers

A personal computer is essentially a machine designed for individual use. It consists of a monitor, system box, keyboard, mouse, various drives, CPU (Central Processing Unit), motherboard and a variety of electronic cards. These components form the main body or computer system but other devices can be connected to it. The most useful of these is probably a printer but there are others such as scanners, digital cameras and joysticks. These external devices are called peripheral devices. Figure 1.7 illustrates a desktop personal computer with the monitor placed on top of the box containing the system. Personal computers can also take the form of a tower with the monitor positioned next to the tower or with the tower placed under the desk. Figure 1.8 shows the front and back of a tower personal computer.

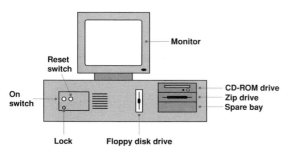

Figure 1.7 Desktop computer

The parts of the computer system that you are able to see may include the following.

◢ A monitor on which the computer information is displayed. They vary in quality which is often expressed in terms of resolution and refresh rate and in size from 14 to 21 inches (i.e. measured across the diagonal of the display). The higher the resolution and refresh rate, the better the monitor.

◢ The system box or unit in which the main components of the computer are stored. These include: CPU (central processing unit), memory, drives and power supply. All the computer components are connected to the system through ports (connectors) which are often located on the back of the unit. Figure 1.8 shows some of the ports.

◢ A CD-ROM or DVD drive which allows the system to read the respective disks on which most software is now supplied. While a CD-ROM can hold 650 megabytes of data, DVD disks can hold gigabytes (i.e. approximately 1000 million bytes) of information and they are gradually superseding CD-ROMs. Both these types of disks enable you to read large volumes of previously stored information but you cannot change or amend the data. There are drives which allow you to store new information on them. They are called CD-R (i.e. Compact Disk Recordable) and CD-RW (i.e. Compact Disk Read Write). CDR allows you to record data once only, while CD-RW allows you to write and rewrite data to the disk many times.

- A Zip drive is a means of storing data on small disks which resemble floppy disks. They hold 100 to 250 megabytes but are not interchangeable with floppy disks. There are a range of devices to allow you to store computer data on removable media such as CD-R and CD-RW. There are also new forms (e.g. Superdisk) of floppy disk which allow you to store many megabytes of information on a single disk.

- A floppy drive is the standard way of moving information between computers. A floppy disk is a small magnetic disk on which a small amount of data can be stored.

The parts of the computer system which are hidden inside the system unit may include the following.

- A Central Processing Unit (CPU) that is the 'brain' of the computer. The speed of the CPU is measured by its clock speed (e.g. Pentium III 700MHz, 800MHz AMD Athlon, and Celeron 300) . This shows how many million times per second a CPU carries out a basic operation. It is measured in MHz (megahertz). There are other factors which influence the speed of the computer such as the actual design of the CPU and the speed the CPU talks to the rest of the computer.

- A graphics card that controls the display of images on the monitor. If you want to display 3D graphics then you normally need a specialist card which is sometimes called an accelerator. This is important if you wish to play games.

- Expansion slots which are places for you to add extra electronic cards to the system in order to increase its functionality (e.g. sound).

- A modem which allows your computer to communicate with other computers. Modems can also be external devices.

- A motherboard which is a circuit board into which all the other components connect so that they can communicate with each other.

- A chipset which is a group of chips on the motherboard which control the main functions of the computer (i.e. allowing the CPU to communicate with memory, hard disk and cards).

- A hard disk which is a magnetic disk on which software and data are stored. It is the main long-term storage area in the system.

- Random Access Memory (RAM) which is the working memory of the computer. It is lost when you switch off the machine.

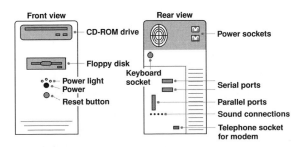

Figure 1.8 Tower Front and Rear Views

Exercise 1.2

Explore a personal computer

Duration 20 minutes

1   On your own personal computer or on another try to identify:

   ◄ if it is a tower or a desktop computer;

   ◄ the monitor (what size is it?);

   ◄ the mouse (how many buttons does it have?);

   ◄ the keyboard;

   ◄ the floppy drive;

   ◄ the zip or CD-R/CD-RW drives (your computer may not have any of these drives);

   ◄ the CD-ROM/DVD drive (your computer may not have any of these drives).

2   Look at the back of the computer and trace with your eyes how the cables link the different parts together. However, do not touch them unless you have first isolated the machine from the power supply. You should be able to identify the links to the keyboard and mouse and perhaps to the printer, external modem, telephone socket and scanner.

3   Try the monitor controls (e.g. brightness, contrast, vertical and horizontal hold) and adjust your display

Optional

4   If possible, you should view the internal components of the computer. However, this should only be done with the support of a computer technician and in every case with the machine both switched off and isolated from the power supply. If you can, identify the following:

   ◄ CPU

   ◄ drives

   ◄ power supply

   ◄ chipset

   ◄ expansion slots

► TUTORIAL 1.3   Output devices

The two main output devices are monitors and printers. A monitor or visual display unit (VDU) is attached to almost all types of personal computers. However, their size varies enormously from a tiny display a few square centimetres on a personal digital assistant to a large display unit attached to a desktop computer. Many monitors resemble a television set and are available in a variety of sizes (e.g. 14in, 15in, 17in and larger). A new design has produced VDUs which are far narrower than traditional monitors. The size of a monitor is measured across the diagonal of the screen. Figure 1.9 illustrates a multimedia monitor in that speakers are attached to the sides. Speakers can be free-standing or built into the system unit. Sound is an important output from multimedia computer systems.

The characteristics of a monitor are determined by its size, resolution and refresh rate. The refresh rate tells you how many times per second the image is redrawn on the screen. If your monitor has a fresh rate below 75hz it will have a noticeable flicker. Refresh rates normally reduce as resolution increases.

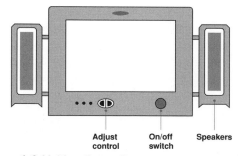

Figure 1.9 Multimedia monitor

Resolution is a measure of how many dots (pixels) make up the image. The greater the resolution, the finer detail that can be displayed. Typical resolutions are 640 x 480, 800 x 600 and 1280 x 1024. A monitor can work with a range of resolutions and the operating system allows you to choose the resolution you prefer. In general, the higher the refresh rate and resolution, the better the quality of image will be displayed.

Printers are a very important means of organising the output of computer information by printing the data on paper. There are currently three main types of printer:

- monochrome laser printer;
- monochrome and colour inkjet printer;
- colour laser printer.

A laser printer uses black magnetic toner very similar to that used in photocopiers to produce text and images on paper. A drum is used to transfer the toner to paper by charging it with static electricity to repel the toner. A laser beam then removes the static charge corresponding to the image or text being printed so that the toner can adhere to the drum and thus be transferred to the paper. Laser printers are widely used in the workplace because of their high quality and speed of output.

Inkjet printers work by squirting small drops of ink on to the page. They can provide both black and white and colour printing. The ink is stored in cartridges which are simple to replace. These types of printers have improved very rapidly in quality and fallen in price so that they are now widely used in the home and in business (e.g. to provide coloured output).

Colour laser printers are still relatively expensive and normally reserved for large or specialist (i.e. printers and graphic designers) business users. However, high-street copying shops often provide colour laser printing for the individual or small business user.

The quality of all printers is normally presented in terms of print resolution expressed in dots per inch (dpi) and speed in terms of pages per minute (ppm). Most printers offer a range of resolutions but often speed will decrease with an increase in resolution. Colour inkjets are frequently slower than black and white. However, the quality and speed of all printers are improving quickly. Typical print resolution ranges from 300 to 1200 dpi while speeds vary from 1 ppm to 40 ppm at the moment.

Exercise 1.3

Explore a printer   Duration 20 minutes

1 Identify the type of printer that you have access to, either in your workplace, at college, at a community learning centre or at home.

2 Explore the machine (after you have isolated it from the power supply) by locating the ink cartridges or toner cartridge. Consider how you would replace the cartridge. Printers often have instructions printed on the machine or the cartridge packaging.

3 Consider how paper is loaded into the printer and its route through the printer.

4 Load paper into the printer and switch it on.

▶ TUTORIAL 1.4 Input devices

The main types of input devices are the keyboard and the mouse, although there are a wide range of other devices including different types of scanner (e.g. flatbed, sheet and pen), pointing devices (e.g. light pens, joysticks, touch pads and roller balls) and speech input.

Figure 1.10 shows a conventional QWERTY keyboard. This is a widely available keyboard like a typewriter which is used on many desktop/tower computers. Other types of keyboard are used on notebook, palmtop and on Apple Macintosh computers. Notebooks (sometimes called laptops) often have pointing devices built into their keyboards. These can take a wide variety of forms such as roller balls, touch pads and buttons.

A mouse is a commonly used means of controlling an on-screen pointing. The pointer allows objects (e.g. icons and buttons) to be chosen in order to initiate an action. There are many different types of mouse. There are mice with one, two or three buttons (see Figure 1.11) but two-button mice are probably the most widely used. Each button works with the operating system or application to produce different effects. The left mouse button is used to select and confirm action while the right button is often reserved to access extra functions. In most cases the movement and button presses are communicated to the computer through a cable connected to a port but some mice use infra-red senders and receivers. Some mice include a roller bar in order to allow them to scroll the display.

The combination of mouse and keyboard is associated with interacting with Graphic User Interfaces (GUI). Most modern software uses a GUI interface (e.g. Microsoft Windows, Apple Macintosh and Microsoft Office applications).

▶ Explore the keyboard

Duration 30 minutes

Exercise 1.4

1 Study the keyboard and try to identify:

   ✦ the number pad which is used when you need to input a large amount of numerical information;

   ✦ function keys – these are often linked to special operations;

   ✦ enter key – this tells computer to action an operation;

   ✦ arrow keys which move the cursor around the screen;

   ✦ other keys such as tab, space bar, CTRL, ALT and ESC keys;

   ✦ different delete keys (there is more than one).

2 Consider the order of the alphanumerical keys (i.e. QWERTY).

3 Identify any special keys (e.g. F1, F9, Page Up, Caps Lock etc.).

There are three main types of scanner (see Figure 1.12):

✦ A flatbed scanner for inputting illustrations and text into the computer.

It looks like a small photocopier and it is used in a similar way. To scan text requires OCR (Optical Character Reading) software that allows the text to be imported into a word-processor so that it can be manipulated.

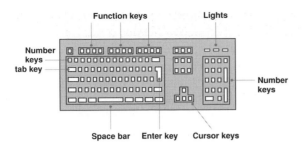

Figure 1.10 Keyboard

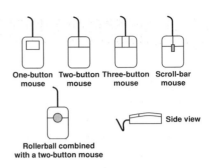

Figure 1.11 Different types of mouse

A sheet scanner which is primarily used to scan text on documents.

A pen scanner which is rather like a highlighting pen in that lines of text can be scanned and stored in the device. The text can then be transferred from the pen into a computer by attaching a cable or by using infra red. Some pen scanners can operate with multiple languages and even output the text as spoken English.

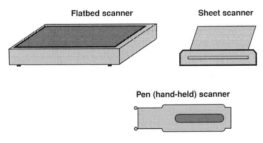

Figure 1.12 Different types of scanner

Although speech input has been available for many years, it has normally required specialist equipment and had a relatively high cost. Recently, however, the cost has fallen dramatically and specialist equipment has been reduced to a simple microphone and some software. This has made speech input available to all computer users. However, the software available normally works best when the system has been trained to the voice of a particular user. This requires the user to repeat a range of words and phrases into the system for it to learn the style of users' speech. Each user of the system must train the system. The main use of speech input has been to produce a document in conjunction with a word-processor. Speech output is also possible where written words can be synthesised through the computers speakers. This has been used to provide systems for visually impaired users so that screen displays are read to them.

TUTORIAL 1.5 Computer memory

A computer needs a place to store and work on information. This is called memory. Computers have several types of memory, a fact which often confuses beginners. These include:

Random Access Memory (RAM). This is working memory in which the computer carries out its functions while it is switched

on. It only exists while the machine is on. If the power is switched off, so is the memory. RAM is very important to the speed and efficiency of the computer. The more RAM it has, the faster the computer will operate. RAM is often allocated to specific tasks, in particular providing memory for graphics which is called video memory.

- Read Only Memory (ROM). This is permanent memory and is built into the structure of the silicon chips inside the computer. It is not lost if the power is switched off.

- Storage. This is where information and programs are stored as magnetic patterns on a hard disk, flash memory card (e.g. in a digital camera), CD-RW, DVD RAM or floppy disk.

When the computer is switched on, it uses ROM to provide the basic instructions to set up the computer. It works on problems in RAM and stores the result on the hard disk, CD-R, CD-RW, magnetic tape or a floppy disk.

All forms of memory are measured in bytes. A byte is sufficient memory to store one character (e.g. a letter or a number). There is a smaller unit of memory called a bit. A byte equals eight bits. A bit is essentially enough memory to store a single item of binary arithmetic, that is, a one or a zero. Modern computers are often described in terms of their memory (e.g. 128 megabytes of RAM). For example:

- 1.44 Megabytes of floppy disk (about 1,440,000 bytes or 1,44 Kb)

- 64 Megabytes of RAM (about 64 million bytes or 64 mb)

- 650 Megabytes CD-R (about 650 million bytes or 650 mb)

- 10 Gigabyte hard disk (about 10,000 million bytes or 10 Gb)

TUTORIAL 1.6 Computer networks

Mainframe computers

The first computers were mainframes. They were very large and powerful machines which required a team of specialist staff to operate and program them. They occupied entire floors of large buildings and required air conditioning and environmental controls in order to function correctly. They undertook large computational tasks such as keeping the accounts for an entire multinational company or government department. For many years they were the only type of computer available and thus few people ever came in contact with them.

People communicate with mainframes through dumb terminals which look similar to personal computers but do not have any processing power of their own. Their purpose is simply to communicate with the mainframe which undertakes all the processing. A mainframe can handle communications with many hundreds of users simultaneously with many of them working in remote sites. Equally, the mainframe can run many different programs at the same time so it is able to multi-task (i.e. perform many different tasks at the same time) with multiple users. Consequently, it is often described as a multi-task and multi-user computer system.

The first computer networks were based around mainframes which many people were using who were often working in geographically remote sites. The network was totally dependent on the mainframe since the individual terminals could only communicate with the central computer. Mainframes are still used extensively today but the trend is to develop systems based around networks of personal computers. Figure 1.13 illustrates a mainframe network.

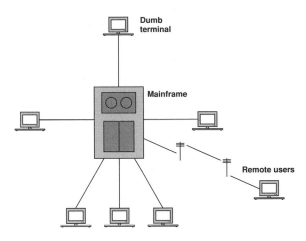

Figure 1.13 Mainframe

Mini-computers

Mainframe computers are suitable for large-scale use involving large groups of users and major tasks. However, if a small enterprise or a single department of a large company requires a computer, mainframes are too expensive and not suitable. Mini-computers were developed to fit this type of use. They are again based around the idea of a central computers with users linked by dumb terminals, but they are far simpler in that they do not require specialist staff to manage them or controlled environments (e.g. air-conditioning) in which to operate.

Mini-computers are used within individual organisations to undertake the functions required by the enterprise (e.g. accounts and storage of customer information). They are far more robust than mainframes so they are used in industrial applications or in locations where mainframes would be uneconomical or impracticable. A single mini-computer and terminals form a computer network but mini-computers can be linked together to extend the network.

Both mainframes and mini-computers are centralised systems where the individual terminals are not able to work independently of them. The personal computer changed this configuration since they are standalone machines. Personal computers can act as terminals, but, in order to do this, they must run emulation software which makes the computer behave like a dumb terminal. It does however add flexibility, since when they are not working with the mini- or mainframe computers, they can process information independently.

The next logical step was to link personal computers together to try to build on the advantage of independent machines. This is especially important with the growth in computer power available to the personal computer. Individual machines can now carry out significant tasks.

Local Area Networks (LANs)

A computer network is a group of computers linked by cables so that they can communicate with each other in order to share resources. Small, single-organisation networks are normally called LANs (Local Area Networks). Local Area Networks are widely used in many different organisations from small businesses to schools. This is because they allow you to maximise the return on your investment in computer equipment. The major benefits are:

- sharing expensive equipment (e.g. printers);

- access to common files and resources;

- communication between users through the use of e-mail.

There are a number of alternative approaches to linking computers together. The two that you will encounter are peer-to-peer and those employing a central computer called a server. In both these cases, there are a number of alternative configurations and combinations of equipment depending on the precise needs of the organisation. Figure 1.14 shows an example of a peer-to-peer network. A peer-to-peer network is simply a collection of individual personal computers. These can be configured in different ways but there are two main choices:

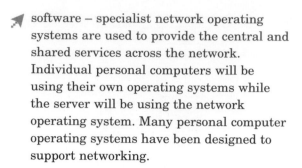

- each computers works independently and does not provide a service to the whole network;

- individual computers become non-dedicated servers in that they can work alone but provide services for the whole network so that other computers can access information stored on them.

Peer-to-peer networks tend to be used for small LANs of 3 – 10 computers. For larger LANs, a central server is used to store common network resources so that everyone can back up their files on to the server and everyone can gain access to standard files and applications. Figure 1.15 shows an example of a client server network.

The main components of a LAN are:

- cabling – this can take many forms ;

- network cards – these have to be installed in each computer to allow them to link to the network cable;

- software – specialist network operating systems are used to provide the central and shared services across the network. Individual personal computers will be using their own operating systems while the server will be using the network operating system. Many personal computer operating systems have been designed to support networking.

Wide Area Networks (WANs)

LANs are often linked together using telecommunication lines over large geographical areas to form WANs (Wide Area Networks). A WAN can cover an individual town, county or even continent. The different LANs are linked together through hardware devices called routers. Routers are linked by high-speed data lines supplied by telecommunication companies such as British Telecom. They are being linked by lines which were originally intended for telephone contacts.

Telecommunication lines vary in their bandwidth which determines the speed of connection. In all networks, the cables linking the computers are critical for their success. When considering a geographically widespread network, the telecommunication lines are the 'glue' that holds it all together. The Internet is a very large worldwide WAN which is totally

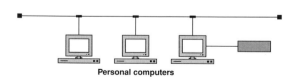

Personal computers

Figure 1.14 Peer-to-peer network

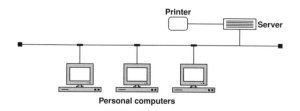

Personal computers

Figure 1.15 Client server network

dependent on all forms of telecommunication lines including those intended for spoken communications.

The world telephone network is called the Public Switched Telephone Network. It is essential for the many home and small organisations who use it to take part in the Internet. It is, however, an analogue system whereas the computer uses digital information. This means that the digital data must be converted to analogue which is done by using a device called a modem. When the data arrives with the other computer, it is converted back to digital. The modem determines the speed of data transmission. Using conventional approaches, normally the highest speed possible is 33.4 Kbps to send and 56.6 Kbps to download information. The speed of transmission is given in Kbps which is thousands of bits per second, a bit being an individual piece of digital information, essentially either one or nought. Another unit of measurement is the baud which is equivalent to a bit per second.

If you need to send data at higher speeds, you need to use special digital lines. Telecommunication companies are able to supply most users with Integrated Services Digital Network (ISDN) lines. These provide a high speed, broadband link which is specially designed for digital data transmission. The basic speed for ISDN is 64 Kbps.

Other options available are Asymetric Digital Subscriber Lines (ADSL) and leased lines which can provide higher speeds. Leased lines can provide very high speed transmission rates but normally at a high cost while ADSL offers you a permanent broadband link through the telephone system. ADSL is regarded as the method to bring high speed broadband links into the home. However, other means of producing broadband links are also being developed including wireless networking. This

allows your laptop computer to communicate with your desktop without using cables.

Internet

The ultimate in networks is the Internet which is a worldwide communication network. It links computers owned by millions of individuals and organisations. It has been growing rapidly for many years in Europe and North America and has now become a truly global phenomenon. The Internet connects almost every possible type of organisation and individual with many people linking to it from their own homes. The Internet consists of a number of different services and components. The Internet allows you to:

- communicate through electronic mail (e-mail) – this provides you with the means of sending and receiving messages to any other e-mail user in the world;

- remotely control another computer – this is achieved using Telnet;

- transfer files between computers connected to the Internet using File Transfer Protocol (FTP);

- communicate with groups and individuals using mailgroups, newsgroups (often called Usenet) and chat – there are many thousands of different groups covering almost every interest, hobby or viewpoint;

- display information on your own World Wide Web (WWW) site or visit other websites to gain information – there are millions of websites available to you and the number is growing, changing and developing rapidly

The World Wide Web

The World Wide Web is part of the Internet. However, it is so large and complex that to many users the WWW is the Internet. A reasonable description is that the Internet is the structure of computers and links while the WWW is the contents. Websites are structured information made available on computers linked to the Internet. Almost every major organisation, multinational company and university have developed websites. These are often very complex, providing visitors with access to large volumes of information. Many individuals have launched their own websites using home computers or the space provided by Internet Service Providers.

E-mail

For many people electronic mail is often the most useful part of the Internet. It allows them to communicate to any other e-mail user in the world. E-mail is a worldwide electronic postal service. Internet Service Providers (ISP) provide e-mail accounts as part of their service to give you access to the Internet. There is no limit to the number of e-mail accounts you can have and many people have a home account, a work account, etc. It is rather like owning many different post office boxes. E-mail has many advantages such as:

- it is very cheap;
- it is possible to send e-mails anywhere in the world in a few minutes;
- it is not limited to text but allows you to send pictures, sounds and video;
- it is possible to send e-mail at any time;

- it allows you to send a message to multiple recipients.

In order to use e-mail you need:

- access to the Internet;
- an e-mail account;
- a modem and connection;
- e-mail software.

Search engines

The scale and rapid growth of the WWW means that it can be difficult to locate particular sites. In order to help you to find sites relating to your interests there are several sites which function to search the WWW for sites that match your interests. These are called search engines. They work by matching keywords with the contents of sites around the WWW. Search engines analyse the WWW sites and store the information on a database so that when you enter your keywords it is a quick process to identify suitable web pages. Most search engines list the pages they locate in the order they judge nearest to the keywords. Search engines can also be used to find newgroup messages and individual e-mail addresses.

There is another form of search engine called a directory. This is a list of sites organised into categories. You search a directory by choosing a broad subject such as athletics and are then presented with a list of choices. After making a series of choices you arrive at the site you want. One of the best known directories is Yahoo (http://www.yahoo.co.uk). Some search engines offer both search facilities and directories. Tutorial 8.3 (Chapter 8) provides a list of search engines and directories.

Networks

Duration 60 minutes

1 If you are studying ECDL at a college, in a learning centre or at work it is very likely that the computer you are using is part of a Local Area Network (LAN). Investigate your network to identify:

- the type of network you are using (e.g. client server);

- the number of terminals which form the network;

- if your terminals are dumb or intelligent;

- where your files are stored (e.g. on the hard disk of your desktop computer, server, mini-computer etc.)

- how your network is linked to the Internet (it may not be connected);

- who manages the network (e.g. system manager).

2 If it is possible, speak to the person responsible for the network and ask him or her to identify the main problems of running the network and what plans the organisation has for its future development. Try in particular to identify why there are problems and reasons for the changes.

Computers and society

By the end of this chapter you should understand:

- the use of computers in work, education, the home and society;
- the health and safety aspects of using a computer;
- how to ensure your computer is protected;
- the legal aspects of using a computer;
- computer viruses.

The chapter is divided into six tutorials which include exercises that will allow you to practise many of the ideas presented in the text. Each exercise indicates how long it should take you to complete. They can be undertaken anywhere you can gain access to a computer – work, college, a local library or at home.

The tutorials in this chapter are as follows:

Tutorial 2.1	Computers in society
Tutorial 2.2	Health and safety
Tutorial 2.3	Protecting your information
Tutorial 2.4	Simple maintenance
Tutorial 2.5	The law
Tutorial 2.6	Computer viruses

TUTORIAL 2.1   Computers in society

Information and communication technologies have been influencing all aspects of our lives for many years and the pace of change is accelerating. The level of computer integration into all aspects of society was demonstrated by the concern over the year 2000 bug and the huge amounts of money invested to solve the problem. The Internet is changing the way we access information, define communities and sell our products. ICT can create new markets while making others obsolete. An ICT business can be valued in hundreds of millions without making a profit. Many traditional values are changing and new methods and ideas emerging. A new information society is evolving.

Across the world, many new businesses are being established which are based on customers accessing the business through the Internet. Customers are able to view products in their homes or at their workplace, order them and pay by credit card. This has allowed the development of e-businesses selling books, music, holidays, homes and computer equipment on the World Wide Web. Both traditional and new enterprises have been launched. The Internet provides a means of accessing a worldwide market but local businesses are also growing. It is now possible to order your groceries from a supermarket's website and have them delivered the next day to your home.

In education and training, computers have been used for many years to provide access to multimedia and other forms of computer-based learning materials, but there are now many new developments based on communication technologies which are accelerating the use of computers in learning. The National Grid for Learning in Great Britain is linking all schools as well as some public libraries and community locations so that access to learning materials, experts, teachers and each other will be easily available. For adult learners, Learndirect (which was initially called the University for Industry) is developing an online service which will provide access to high-quality learning through a network of centres and also from learners' homes and work. In addition to these national developments, many Further Education colleges and universities in all parts of the world are offering online courses. These new courses are developing educational providers who can offer learning to anywhere in the world. It is only a matter of time before a true global university or college will emerge.

Computers are now a regular part of people's daily life. You can now design your ideal kitchen, bathroom or garden using computer applications either at home or in the relevant shop. In public libraries, you can search the collection to find any book or journal as well as accessing local information on public access computers. In railway stations, computer-based kiosks are now available to help travellers plan their journeys and familiarise themselves with the new location.

Computers have already had a significant impact on the working life of most people. Most office workers will now use a word-processor to write letters, minutes and notes, spreadsheets to plan project finances and have access to a database of customer information. Engineers will program computer-controlled machine tools to manufacture parts which they have designed using Computer Aided Design (CAD) systems. Photographers employ digital cameras to take photographs which they manipulate with paint applications to remove blemishes and enhance their images. In garages, mechanics will seek spare parts on a computerised stock control system while seeking technical information from the manufacturers' CD-ROM workshop manual.

Most jobs already involve information and communication technologies in some way and the pace of change is such that it is expected that the vast majority of jobs will require workers who are competent computer users.

There are now many applications available for home users including those operating small businesses from their homes. You can also plan your finances including calculating your income tax, index your collection of videos, research your family tree and many other hobbies and interests. In the home, the growth in ownership of computers and links to the Internet has been rapid. However, ownership tends to reflect the financially well-off so there is considerable danger that ownership of information and communication technologies will be a force for social exclusion. In Great Britain, however, there are several initiatives to provide widespread public access to information and communication technologies for people who are socially disadvantaged. This will contribute to ensuring a unified society.

▶ Society Exercise 2.1

Duration 45 minutes

1 Undertake a small survey of your colleagues at work about their personal ownership of computers and whether they have access to the Internet at home.

2 Home ownership and Internet access are growing rapidly and appears to be linked to income,

children and which part of the country you live in. You are more likely to own a computer if you are a high earner, if you have children and if you live in London or South-east England.

3 Ask your colleagues why they bought a computer and connected it to the Internet. Surveys indicate

that this is often related to keeping up to date, helping owners' children and improving job prospects.

4 See if you can identify any social issues among your colleagues linked to computer ownership and access to the Internet.

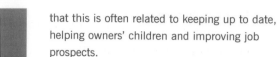

TUTORIAL 2.2 Health and safety

There is a range of issues to consider in order to provide a safe and healthy working environment for yourself and others when using a computer. The main factors are:

- Lighting – the screen will reflect light so when you are using the computer you may find screen glare unpleasant. It is important to position the computer so that office lights or the sun will not be reflected. It is normally effective to position your computer at right angles to any windows. You should adjust the brightness, contrast and tilt of the monitor to meet your needs.

- Breaks – it is poor practice to work at a computer for long periods without a break. You should take regular breaks away from the machine.

- Posture – it is important to position yourself in a relaxed and comfortable way when working on a computer. You need to ensure that your feet are placed flat on the floor or on a footrest and that you are directly facing the computer screen. You should not have to twist or turn to see your papers or to use the computer. It should always feel pleasant and comfortable. If you have to strain even slightly then re-position your machines to remove the strain.

- Space – you need to have adequate working space around your computer for your materials (e.g. papers, books and telephone) so that you do not have to stretch, over-reach or twist to use them. If you are even slightly uncomfortable then change the layout until you are comfortable.

- Seating – your chair should be adjustable and you should alter the height and backrest to suit you. It is important that your lower back is supported by the chair and your feet are placed on the floor or on a foot rest with the knees slightly higher than the chair to ensure good circulation of blood. The height of the chair should be adjustable to allow your eyes to be slightly below the top of the screen and you should view the screen from a distance of at least 18 inches.

- Repetitive strain injury is a real problem for computer users. It needs to be prevented by ensuring that users are able to work in a relaxed and comfortable way. You can reduce the strain on hands and wrists by keeping your wrists straight while typing (e.g. by using an arm rest), avoiding resting on your wrists (i.e. do not put a strain on your wrists or arms), type gently without excessive force and avoid typing for long periods. In all cases, if you are uncomfortable or your arms, fingers, wrist, shoulders or hands feel tired or strained, then check your position. Something is wrong.

Check your position Duration 15 minutes

1 Review the layout and position of your personal computer workplace or, if you don't have one, use the college, home or learning centre layout where you are studying. Consider screen glare, space, chair and posture.

2 Are you comfortable when using the computer?

3 How long do you normally work on the computer without a break?

TUTORIAL 2.3 Protecting your information

In the past the security of information was achieved by the complexity of the files and by locking filing cabinets and rooms. It was difficult for someone not familiar with the filing system to locate a particular file. However, it is now possible for a single person to delete the information by entering the wrong commands or by a hard disk crashing. While, the computer provides a powerful means of organising and using information, it is also relatively easy to lose information accidentally or to have information accessed by people who are not authorised to see it. It is important to protect your files against both accidental and deliberate loss or misuse.

Protection against accidental loss is normally achieved by copying the files and storing them in a location away from the computer. There is a wide range of backup devices depending on the system you are using. A local area network may store information on each computer's hard disk while backing up the data on the network server and copying the server's files on to magnetic tape. In this way, information is stored in three locations. However, a fire might destroy all three sets of information, so the magnetic tape is often stored in either a fire-proof safe or in a location outside the workplace. An individual computer's files can be stored (backed up) on a variety of devices including floppy disks, removable hard disks, optical disks, zip drives and magnetic tape.

Operating systems (e.g. Microsoft Windows) provide standard back-up functions both to copy files to a removable media and also to restore the files to the computer.

Example

In Microsoft Windows, the back-up functions are located by clicking on Start button, highlighting Programs, selecting Accessories, System Tools and Backup. Figure 2.1 illustrates the Backup function.

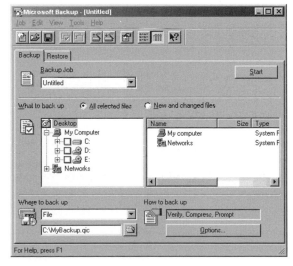

Figure 2.1 Backup function

Backing up data prevents accidental loss but it does not prevent unauthorised use of the computer or people improperly using your information. To do this requires additional security measures. The most used means of controlling access to a computer is by passwords. This ensures that you can limit access to authorised personnel. Figure 2.2 shows the password functions provided by Microsoft Windows.

The process of providing everyone with an initial password is not sufficient for continuing protection. Passwords must be kept secret from other users. They must be changed regularly to ensure that other people cannot guess them. It is important that users are instructed to memorise their password and not write it down so that others can find it. They must not share their passwords with other users or pick an obvious password but rather one which is difficult to guess. To summarise:

- Change passwords frequently.

- Choose passwords that others who know you cannot guess. It is good practice to include numbers, different case letters and symbols within the password. This will make it harder to crack.

- Memorise passwords. Do not keep a written record of them.

It is possible to establish different types of password so that different users are given access to different functions. This allows general users to have access to standard applications such as word-processing, spreadsheets, database and e-mail while not being able to change the system settings or access the network server. The system administrator, in contrast, can be given a password which allows him or her to change system settings. This hierarchy of password access is another means of ensuring the security of the system.

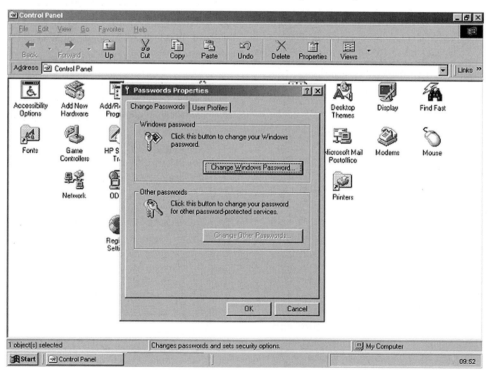

Figure 2.2 Password protection

Exercise 2.3

Security   Duration 15 minutes

1   Identify the security systems employed within   ↗ who can override individual passwords;
    your own organisation or where you are studying.
                                                          ↗ who controls network security;
2   In particular discover:
                                                          ↗ how often passwords are changed.
    ↗ who decides on passwords;

TUTORIAL 2.4   Simple maintenance

There is a range of simple straightforward actions you can take which will protect your equipment, yourself and others. These include the following:

↗ Regularly dusting your equipment and cleaning the monitor screen. There are screen wipes and other products designed to clean the screen but you must only dust the rest of the hardware. You should avoid aerosols since these can harm the electronic components of the computer.

↗ Keeping your floppy disks out of direct sunlight and away from any magnetic source since it will destroy your data. It is good practice to keep floppy disks in their box when they are not is use.

↗ Keeping all air vents free of obstructions on your computer, printer, monitor etc. or the equipment may overheat and be damaged.

↗ Not moving the computer while it is switched on since this may damage your hard disk. When you close down the computer using the operating system commands, it will park the hard disk.

↗ Using the operating system's procedure for closing down your system safely. If you

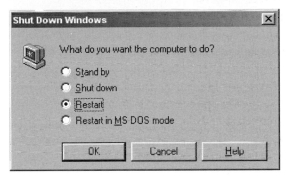

Figure 2.3 Microsoft Windows Shut Down

simply switch off the computer while applications are still running then you may corrupt your files. Figure 2.3 shows the Shut Down display for Microsoft Windows.

↗ Avoiding eating or drinking near a computer. Mixing liquids with electrical equipment is very dangerous.

↗ Keeping your cables tidy. The different components of a computer system are linked by a range of cables and frequently each have a separate power cable which leads to the risk of people tripping over them and injuring themselves.

Simple maintenance Duration 20 minutes

Exercise 2.4

1 Switch your computer off and isolate the computer from the electricity supply.

2 Investigate the cables which connect the different components of your system. Even if you have a very basic computer system it is likely to have a lot of cables hidden behind your machine.

3 Trace each cable to identify which components are liked together. Try to identify the power cables, printer leads, network connection, mouse and keyboard cables and monitor lead.

4 Ensure that the cables present no risk to anyone else.

TUTORIAL 2.5 The law

When you buy a program, you are essentially buying a licence to use the application. The program remains the property of its producer. The licence imposes a number of conditions on you. If you break them, you are infringing the producer's copyright. In many cases, the licence only allows you to install the software on a single computer and to make one backup copy. The conditions of each user licence will vary between products so you must read them to ensure you do not breech them.

You can also buy a network version of a program which provides you with a licence allowing multiple simultaneous users. However, the price increases with the number of users (i.e. 5, 10, 25, 100 etc.). It is also possible to purchase a site licence for an application which allows unlimited use but limited to a single location. This type of licence is often bought by large companies, universities and government departments. Software producers also offer different types of licence for different types of users. This normally means a lower price for educational organisations and in some cases teachers and students.

Illegal copying of software is called piracy and costs the industry millions of pounds annually. If you make an illegal copy, you are committing an offence. You should never copy software

unless the licence permits you to do so.

There are three other forms of software apart from commercial applications. These are:

- shareware
- freeware
- public domain

Shareware is a system by which you are able to try software before you buy it. For a small administration fee, you are provided with a copy of the application to test. If you find it useful and continue to use the product, you are required to register your ownership. This requires you to pay a fee but in return you normally receive an updated version of the application, in some cases technical support and occasionally a manual. Shareware is often distributed over the Internet. It is like commercial software in that your use is still governed by a user licence.

Freeware is both free in price and free of restrictions so that any licence associated with it would often only stipulate that the original author be accredited. Freeware is also referred to as 'Open Source' software in that the original source code is available for adaptation and development. Open Source software is not limited to small applications but includes large products such as operating systems. Technical support is not normally available for open source software except in an informal way through mailgroups and other users of the material.

Public domain software is entirely free of conditions and users can use the software in any way they choose. The producers have essentially given away their product. There is often confusion between the three types of software. It is important to check what category the software is in, since you may be infringing the user licence.

User Licences

Duration 15 minutes

Exercise 2.5

Identify the user licence for an application which you use. This normally forms part of the application manuals. It is good practice to keep all the software documentation in a central library since this ensures that it is easy to locate for the whole organisation. Read the licence to make yourself familiar with the conditions.

One further legal aspect of using computers is covered in the Data Protection Act 1998. Computers are very good at correlating and sharing information about all subjects including personal information. This brings the risk of individual privacy being invaded and your individual privacy being damaged by the misuse of this personal information. To provide legal protection, the European Union has adopted laws which in Great Britain take the form of the Data Protection Act 1998.

The Act requires all organisations who hold or plan to hold personal information on a computer to register with the Office of the Data Protection Registrar. However, if you have a personal address book for your own use you are exempt from registering but if you use the address book for your employer, a club or other organisation the organisation must register. The registration limits the uses to which you can put the information and requires you to secure the data. For further information you can contact the Data Protection Registrar at:

Springfield House
Water Lane
Wilmslow
Cheshire SK9 5AX

Data Protection Registration

Duration 15 minutes

Exercise 2.6

For your own organisation locate the Data Protection Registration and see what the conditions are for holding personal information.

Viruses are pieces of software which are designed to replicate themselves and to damage your computer system. They can delete your files, change your computer settings and fill up your storage with rubbish. In many ways they behave in similar ways to biological viruses. Computer viruses hide themselves within other programs so that by loading what appears to be a perfectly normal program, you are infecting your system with a virus. As soon as you run the host program the virus goes into action. Some viruses wait for a particular date (e.g. Friday, 13th) before beginning to vandalise your system. Others work immediately. The Love Bug was spread by an e-mail attachment and once a computer was infected it sent further e-mails to infect other systems.

You should take great care to load only programs from reputable sources on to your system. Viruses always try to spread themselves so that every time a floppy disk is inserted into an infected computer or an e-mail sent, there is the potential for transferring the virus to another machine. Never load a program unless you are certain it is free from infection. This will substantially reduce the risk of a virus attack. However, it will not completely eliminate the danger. You must take additional precautions in the form of anti-virus software. This will provide substantial protection in detecting and removing viruses. Anti-virus programs can scan programs to check for virus infection and remove it once it is detected. You can set up the software so that it automatically checks files and the whole system.

Viruses normally hide themselves in executable files (i.e. those ending with .exe), self-extracting archives and files which contain a macro (e.g. Microsoft Word). However, if you

are unsure of what files viruses inhabit, check them all. There are thousands of different viruses with more being written all the time. It is therefore vital to update your anti-virus protection regularly. Most suppliers provide a free updating services for customers. This is often in the form of downloading files from the supplier's website.

Viruses are designed to reproduce themselves and to spread their infection. It is therefore critical not to transfer files by any means from any computer which is infected since you will almost certainly infect other computers. If a virus contaminates a computer which is part of a network, there is high probability that you will infect the whole network. Anti-virus programs are available for network use. Many organisations also take other measures to reduce the risk of virus infections. These include:

- testing all programs on an isolated computer before loading them on to the network;

- instructing staff that they should not use any floppy disk from outside the organisation;

- removing floppy and CD-ROM drives from computers to prevent loading of programs by unauthorised staff;

- limiting access to the Internet to prevent downloading of files.

▶ **Virus protection**   **Duration 30 minutes**

1 For you own organisation find out how it protects itself against virus attack.

2 Identify:

🖱 the virus protection software that your organisation uses;

🖱 your organisation rules about loading or downloading software on to the computer system;

🖱 how often your organisation updates its virus protection.

3 Ask your computer or network manager about their experience of virus attacks, problems that these caused and how they rectified them.

Using a computer

1 2 ✓3 4 5 6

By the end of this chapter you should understand:

- how to start and shut down a computer;
- the basic functions of the operating system;
- the structure and interface of the system;
- the way files are stored on the system;
- the different types of files;
- how to maintain, manipulate, organise and restructure files;
- use basic applications.

The chapter covers Module 1 of the ECDL syllabus. It is divided into five tutorials which include exercises that will allow you to practise many of the ideas presented in the text. Each exercise indicates how long it should take you to complete. They can be undertaken anywhere you can gain access to a computer – work, college, a local library or at home.

The tutorials in this chapter are as follows:

▶ TUTORIAL 3.1 Operating system

The Microsoft Windows operating system is normally loaded automatically when you switch on the computer. If you watch the screen, you will see a series of messages appear. These indicate that the hardware is being checked, device drivers are being loaded and the operating system made ready. After a few moments you will be presented with a dialogue box which asks you to enter your user name and password if you have set one up. The Microsoft Windows Desktop will then appear. This is shown in Figure 1.1 (p. 2). Exercise 1.1 (p. 2) provides you with the opportunity to explore the Microsoft Windows operating system environment.

There is often more than one way of carrying out a task such as loading an application using an operating system like Microsoft Windows.

In Figure 3.1 you will see a standard way of loading applications. Clicking on the Start button will cause a menu to pop up. If you place your mouse over the Programs item, it will highlight (i.e. change colour) and a new menu will appear alongside. If you slide your mouse across to the new menu you can move it up and down until you reach the application you want to load. If you want to load Windows Explorer you must place your mouse pointer over this item and click the left mouse button. Windows Explorer will then load.

If the item has a small black triangle next to it, this indicates that there is another menu which will appear as soon as you highlight the item (i.e. position your pointer over the item without clicking).

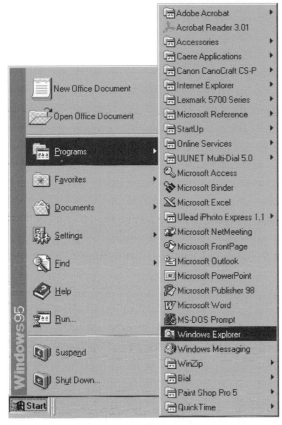

Figure 3.1 Loading Windows Explorer

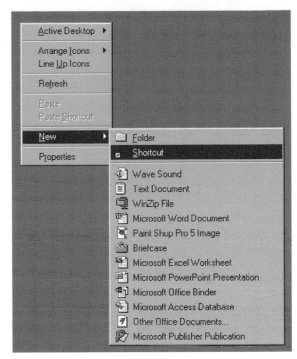

Figure 3.2 Create a Desktop Shortcut

An alternative way of loading an application involves creating a Desktop short cut by placing an icon on the Desktop which, when you click on it, will load the application. This is useful when it is an application which you use frequently.

To create a Desktop shortcut for Windows Explorer (Figure 3.2), right click on Desktop and position your mouse pointer over the New item. This will open a new menu from which you should click on Shortcut. This will reveal a window called Create Shortcut and you need to click on the Browse button, click on the Windows folder, scroll right and double click on the Explorer icon. This will select Explorer and a shortcut can be placed on the desktop by

clicking the Next button and then Finish button. Figure 3.3 illustrates the Explorer icon on the desktop (i.e. the shortcut).

Figure 3.3 Windows Explorer Desktop Shortcut

If you want to remove a shortcut, you need to right click on the icon and a menu will appear with the option Delete. You can remove the icon by selecting and clicking on Delete.

Loading an application Duration 30 minutes

Exercise 3.1

1 Establish a shortcut on the Desktop for Windows Explorer and load it by clicking on the shortcut. Close the application by clicking on the File menu and then on the Close option.

2 Using the Start and Program method load Windows Explorer. Close the application by

clicking on the File menu and then on the Close option or click on the button marked 'X' in the top right of the window.

3 Continue until you are confident about the process.

The two methods of loading described can be used for all types of applications within Microsoft Windows. There is a third approach which is based on finding the location where the programs (application files) are stored. On the Desktop is an icon called My Computer (Figure 3.4)

Figure 3.4 My Computer icon

If you click on the My Computer icon you are presented with a view of the disks attached to the computer, communication links and a folder containing the printer data. However, we will only consider the disks at the moment (i.e. floppy, hard and CD-ROM). The My Computer folder is illustrated in Figure 3.5.

Figure 3.5 shows the three main disks of a personal computer which are:

◄ floppy disk also called the A: drive;

◄ hard disk also called the C: drive;

◄ CD-ROM disk also called the D: drive.

It is possible to have several other drives such as E:, F: etc. If you click on A: then the contents of the floppy disk will be shown in a window. Figure 3.6 illustrates a floppy disk storing four image files. However, this does assume you have a floppy disk in the drive. If you do not then an error message (Figure 3.7) will be displayed.

Floppy disks and other magnetic disks need to be formatted in order to make them suitable to sort files. When you buy a computer the hard

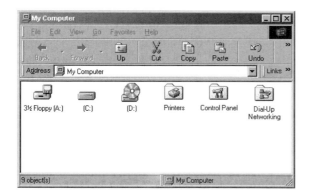

Figure 3.5 My Computer: contents of folder

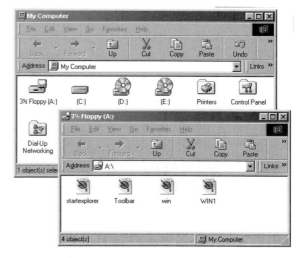

Figure 3.6 Floppy Disk

disk is already formatted for sorting files and you should not reformat it since it will destroy all the data stored on the disk. However, sometimes you need to format a floppy disk although it is normal for disks to be supplied formatted. The Windows operating system provides you with a system for formatting a floppy disk. This is available from the File menu within the My Computer folder. The menu provides an option called Format when the floppy disk is highlighted (i.e. single click on the floppy disk icon within My Computer). By clicking on the Format option you will open a window (Figure 3.8). Click on the Start button in this window to begin formatting the floppy disk.

Figure 3.7 Floppy disk error message

If you click on drive C: then you will be shown what files and folders are stored on the hard disk (Figure 3.9). If you then click on any of the files or folders shown, it will open a new window revealing the sub-folders and files within the main folder. If you click on a program file then the application loads. However, it is often difficult to identify any one file among the large number of other files and folders.

Figure 3.10 shows the structure of folders and files on the hard disk. By clicking on a folder, you move down the structure. You can return by using the Up icon on the toolbar of the window. This reveals the nature of the structure of folders and files. Each level can hold both folders and files. Figure 3.11 illustrates the hierarchical nature of the folders and file structure. Microsoft Windows uses the term 'folder' as the feature in which files and other folders are stored. However, other operating systems use different terms. The main alternative to a folder is a directory, so in other systems you may see the term directory used instead of folder.

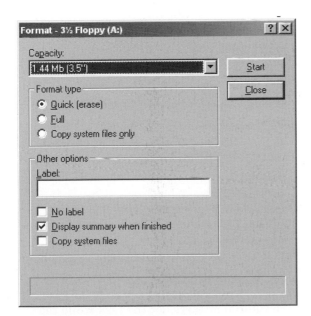

Figure 3.8 Formatting a floppy disk

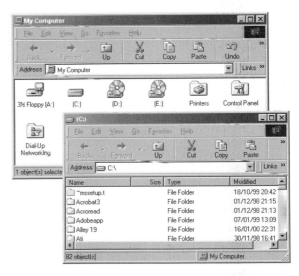

Figure 3.9 Hard disk (C:)

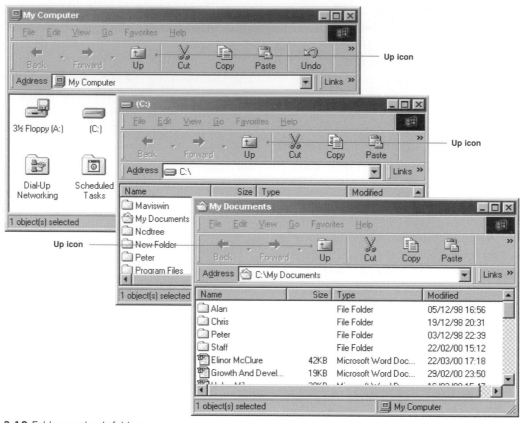

Figure 3.10 Folders and sub-folders

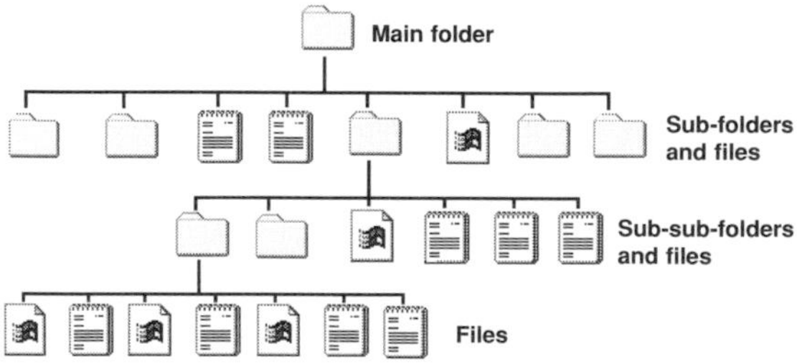

The Windows operating system provides you with its own help system to assist you to use it. The <u>H</u>elp function is available from the Start menu. If you click on <u>H</u>elp then a window opens which provides you with three ways of accessing the contents. These are:

- a list of main content subjects;
- a search for a topic;
- an index of the topics.

You can locate assistance using any of these methods. Topics are often broken down into many sub-topics so you can obtain detailed help with many subjects. The help is provided in the form of short tutorials which explain precisely what you need to do. You can print each tutorial or carry out the task while the tutorial remains on the screen.

Figure 3.11 Folder and file hierarchical structure

▶ TUTORIAL 3.2 Windows

All modern operating systems are based around the concept of windows. Windows are rectangular areas of the display in which information can be shown and applications can run (Figure 3.12). It is possible to have many windows open at any one time so that several applications or a mixture of information and applications can run simultaneously. In order to use Microsoft Windows it is important to understand how to use windows.

All windows have standard features for changing their size and shape. If you position the mouse pointer over any window edge, a double-headed arrow will appear which, if you

hold down the left mouse button, lets you change the size of the window by dragging the edge. In the top right-hand corner of the window are three small icons (Figure 3.13). The left-hand icon allows you minimise the window to an icon on the bottom of the Desktop. You can have many windows minimised. To expand the icon back to a window just click on the icon. The middle icon either expands a small window to fill the entire screen or, if your window is already expanded, reduces it back to a small window. The final icon closes the window and any application running in the window.

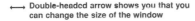
Double-headed arrow shows you that you can change the size of the window

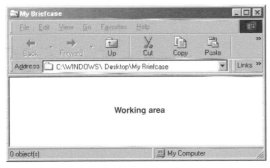

Figure 3.12 A Window

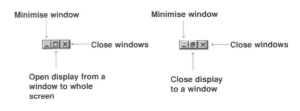

Figure 3.13 Manipulating windows

▶ TUTORIAL 3.3 File structure

Within Microsoft Windows, files are organised and stored within a series of folders and sub-folders. The Windows Explorer application shows the structure of folders, sub-folders and files on the computer. Figure 3.14 shows the structure of a computer's hard disk. In the left-hand side of the display you can see the overall structure of drive C: (i.e. the hard disk). On the right-hand side of the display the sub-folders and files stored within a chosen folder are

shown. In this case the folder is Book which is indicated by the folder being open and the title bar (e.g. Exploring – Book). Book is a sub-folder of the My Documents folder. Folders are opened simply by clicking on them. The plus sign indicates that the folder contains sub-folders. A negative sign indicates that the next level of sub-folders is revealed. There is no limit to the number of folders which can be stored one within the other. Book is a sub-

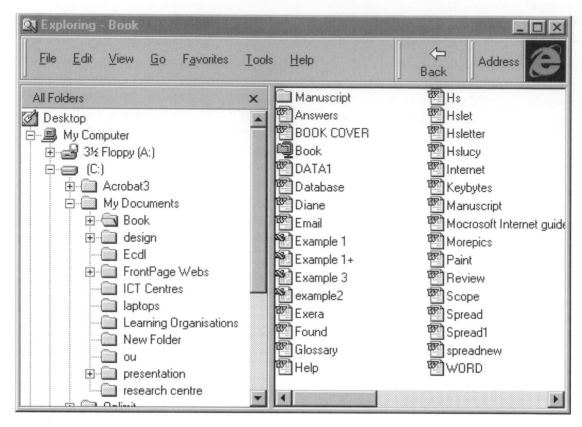

Figure 3.14 Windows Explorer

folder of the My Document folder and Manuscript (see right-hand display) is a sub-folder within Book.

In Microsoft Windows, a folder is shown by a small icon which looks like a cardboard file which, when open, indicates that the folder is revealing its contents of sub-folders and files. Individual files are shown by small icons usually accompanied by a brief description depending on the type of file they contain. Figure 3.15 shows the icons for open and closed folders and some different file types (e.g. word-processing, spreadsheet, database, presentation and image files). File icons vary, depending on the application which created them.

Although we have concentrated on the display of folders and files in terms of their appearance as icons, it is possible to change the display of

Figure 3.15 Files and folders

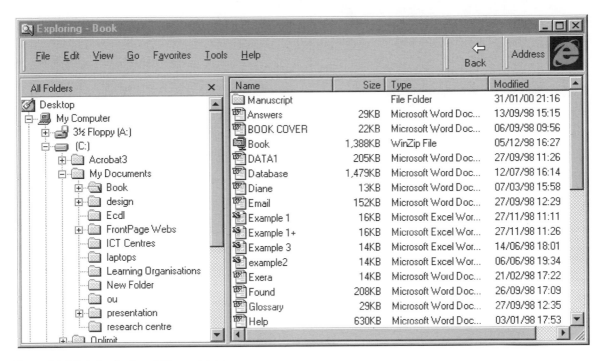

Figure 3.16 Details display of files and folders

folders and files. Figure 3.16 shows the Details display. The other three displays are Large Icons, Small Icons and List. The Details display provides you with a view of the file attributes of name, size, file type and date last modified.

The view of the files and folders is altered using the View menu item. By opening this menu, you are presented with the four choices of Large Icons, Small Icons, List and Details (see Figure 3.17). The display is changed by clicking on any of these four choices.

Figure 3.17 View Menu

1 Open Windows Explorer by clicking on the Start

Creating a hierarchy of folders

Duration 60 minutes

button, selecting <u>P</u>rograms and then clicking on Windows Explorer. You will see views similar to Figures 3.1 and 3.2 respectively.

2 Click on <u>F</u>ile in Windows Explorer and a menu will drop down. The first item is called <u>N</u>ew which, if selected, will produce a new menu to the side of the original menu with an item called <u>F</u>older at the top (see Figure 3.18). This is called a slide off menu

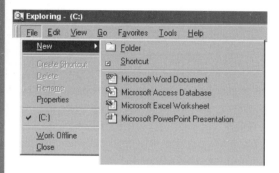

Figure 3.18 New Folder

3 Click on <u>F</u>older and a folder will appear in the right-hand side of the display called New Folder. The title of the folder (i.e. New Folder) is highlighted so you merely need to type over it and enter a new title, 'Test'. The folder has been inserted within whatever folder you already had opened. If you double click on Test you will open the new folder and you can insert a sub-folder by repeating the action (i.e. select <u>N</u>ew and click on <u>F</u>older). Name this file Test1. Insert another sub-folder inside Test1 called Test2. On the left-hand side of the display you will see the hierarchy similar to Figure 3.19.

Figure 3.19 Folder structure

4 You will need to be careful where you insert a new folder. It will be placed in the folder you currently have open.

5 If you make a mistake Windows Explorer provides a number of useful functions. You can change the name of the folder and of individual files. It is also possible to delete, copy, and move files and folders. We will consider moving and copying files in the next tutorial.

6 A folder can be deleted by first of all highlighting it by clicking once. The folder changes colour to indicate that it has been highlighted. You can then delete the folder by pressing either the Delete keys on the keyboard, by clicking on the Delete option within the <u>F</u>ile menu or by right clicking on the folder and selecting Delete option from the drop down menu. The same process is needed if you need to delete a file. Try to delete the Test2 folder. Whatever means you choose to delete a file or a folder (i.e. <u>F</u>ile menu, Delete keys or right clicking) then a window appears asking you to confirm your decision. This is shown in Figure 3.20 When you click on <u>Y</u>es, the folder or file will be removed. You can still recover the file or folder by using the <u>U</u>ndo option in the <u>E</u>dit menu. Practise deleting and undoing the action.

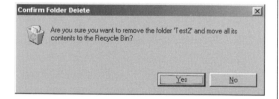

Figure 3.20 Confirm Delete

7 Undo is an excellent method of recovering if you immediately realise that you have made an error. An hour later, it may not be available to you. Nevertheless, you can still recover if you have

made an error, since the folder or file will have been moved to a special area called the Recycle Bin. It remains there until you choose to empty this bin, so it is possible to return a folder or file. The Recycle Bin is usually positioned on the Microsoft Windows Desktop and you access it by clicking on the icon shown in Figure 3.21 This will open the application window shown in Figure 3.22

Figure 3.21 Recycle Bin icon

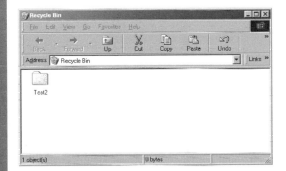

Figure 3.22 Recycle Bin

8 To restore the file or folder, you must initially click on it to highlight the icon. If you then click on the File menu item you will see a menu with an option called Restore. By clicking on Restore, the folder or file is returned to wherever it was deleted from. However, if you do not highlight the folder or file when you open the File menu you will find no option to Restore. Explore the Recycle Bin and see how it works by returning Test2.

9 Another important function is renaming a folder or file. This can be carried out within Windows Explorer by highlighting the folder of your choice. So highlight Test2 which you have just restored and click on File menu item then click on Rename option. The name below the folder is enclosed in a rectangular box and you can enter a new name. When you have finished typing the new name press enter or left click your mouse.

10 Try to rename Test2.

11 Close Windows Explorer.

▶ TUTORIAL 3.4 Creating, saving and printing a file

Although Microsoft Windows is an operating system, it includes a number of applications which it calls Accessories. These include a straightforward text editor or simple word-processor called Wordpad. Wordpad is located within the Program menu on the Accessories menu (Figure 3.23).

Accessories also provides a painting and drawing application (Windows Paint), another text editor (Notepad), a calculator, address book and a variety of other tools. When you click on Wordpad then the application is loaded (Figure 3.24). If you click in the work area you

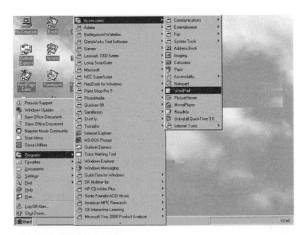

Figure 3.23 Accessories

▶

can enter text which will appear in the font and character size as indicated by Wordpad. Wordpad has many of the features that powerful word-processors provide such as menu and toolbars which allow you to save files, print and change the layout of the document (e.g. left, centre and right justification of the text).

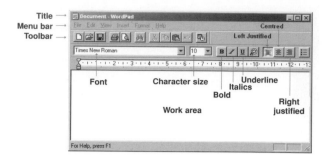

Figure 3.24 Wordpad

Wordpad Duration

Duration 60 minutes

Exercise 3.3

1 Load Wordpad by clicking on Start, selecting Programs and Accessories and click on Wordpad. Figure 3.24 illustrates Wordpad running in a window. Maximise the application using the button in the right-hand corner of window unless it is already full screen.

2 Click in the work area of Wordpad and enter the text below:

This is a new text file that I am creating in Wordpad which is a straightforward text editor provided as part of Microsoft Windows.

3 Once you have entered the text, you need to save it to a folder. You save files by clicking on File and a menu will drop down with the option Save. Click on Save and a small window will appear shown in Figure 3.25. This shows you the current folder, in this case 'My Documents'. Your window will probably show another folder. You can save the text file you have just created by simply entering a file name in File name box (this box is known as a field), clicking within the box and typing in the name. Call your file Padfile. If you next click on the Save button then your file will be saved in the folder showing in the Save in box (e.g My Documents). However, do not save your file yet.

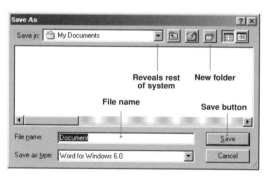

Figure 3.25 Save As Window

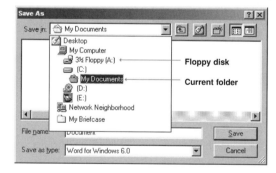

Figure 3.26 Save As window showing drop-down list of folders and disks

4 To the right of the Save in box is a button with a small black triangle pointing down. Click on the button and you will see a simple hierarchy of folders and disks appear similar to those shown in Figure 3.26. It will include 3½ Floppy [A:] which indicates the floppy disk. Insert a floppy into the

drive and then click on this option. You will hear the disk drive engage and the window display will change to show what files if any are already present on the floppy disk and in the Save in box will appear the name 3½ Floppy (see Figure 3.27). Click on the Save button and your file Padfile will be saved on to the disk. You will hear the disk drive. When the process is complete, the Save As window will disappear and you will return to the Wordpad application.

Figure 3.27 Saving files to a floppy disk

5 The Padfile you have created can be printed out. Click on File again and a menu will drop down with the option Print. If you click on Print then the Print window appears shown in Figure 3.28. This shows the default printer (i.e. the printer

which the computer is set up to use) in the Name box. Microsoft Windows allows you to link several printers to your computer. If you click on the button with the small black triangle to the right of the Name box, a drop-down list of other printers or related devices will appear. To change the default printer you only need to click on any other printer listed.

6 Print Padfile using the default printer and then using another listed printer.

7 Microsoft Windows provides a print manager application so that you can monitor a print job's progress. This is very useful if you are sharing a printer with other users (i.e. your printing has to queue up with other documents waiting to use the printer) or if your document is not printed (i.e. something has gone wrong). To access the Print Manager you must click on Start and then select Settings. A menu will appear with Printers as an option. To access the Print Manager, click on it. A window appears with each printer represented by an individual icon. The icon of the printer that the computer is set up to use at that moment will have a tick next to it. By clicking on the icon, you access the Print Manager (see Figure 3.29) for that printer.

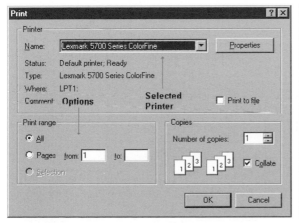

Figure 3.28 Printing a file

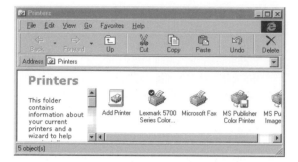
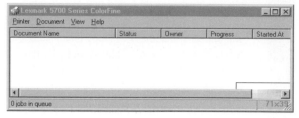

Figure 3.29 Print Manager

TUTORIAL 3.5   Moving, copying and deleting files and folders

Microsoft Windows provides you with a variety of tools to help you manipulate files and folders. The first essential is to locate them. After using a computer for a few months you will probably have hundreds or even thousands of files on your hard disk. It is almost impossible to remember where each of them is stored or even their full names. In the Start menu is an option called Find which, if selected, opens a menu with an option called Files and Folders. Click on this option and the Find window opens (Figure 3.30).

You can use the Find window to search for the name of a file or folder, or text contained in a file. You can search an entire disk (i.e. floppy or harddisk), a particular folder or a group of folders. Figure 3.30 shows that the window has two additional tabs (i.e. Date and Advanced) which allow you to search for files or folders using different methods than simply the name of the file or folder. Date provides you with the means to search for files or folders created between particular dates. Advanced provides you with a means of searching for files or folders by their types (e.g. text, image and spreadsheet files) and also by the size of the file or folder.

Files and folders can be moved from one folder to another by using the options available within Edit. If you click on Edit, the drop-down

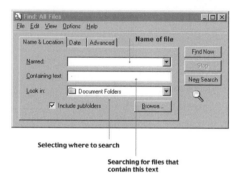

Figure 3.30 Find function

menu reveals options for Cut, Copy and Paste (Figure 3.31). If you highlight a folder or a file by single clicking on it then you can use these options either to Cut (remove file or folder) or Copy (make an extra copy of file or folder). Using the Paste option in the Edit menu, you can then move the file or folder to another folder.

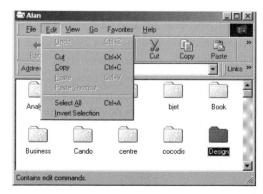

Figure 3.31 Cut, Copy and Paste

Exercise 3.4

Move/copy a file Duration

Duration 30 minutes

1 Insert the floppy disk on which you saved Padfile earlier.

2 From the desktop double click on the My Computer icon to open the window and then on the floppy disk icon to reveal the files stored on your floppy disk. Figure 3.32 shows a floppy disk with only Padfile stored on the disk.

3 There are two methods of moving and copying files. Try both and decide which you are more comfortable with.

4 Method 1:

If you click on the Edit menu item you will see that the three options of Cut, Copy and Paste are all greyed out (i.e. the colour is very faint) which indicates these options are not available. This is because you have not yet highlighed a file or folder to act on. If you click on Padfile to highlight it then the options Cut and Copy are shown in full colour indicating that they are available. However, Paste is still greyed out since the Paste function is only available once you have carried out a Cut or Copy. With Padfile highlighted, click on Cut and Padfile file will fade to show you are moving it. If you click on Edit and then Paste you will see an error message telling you that you cannot move a file with the same source and destination. However, Padfile's colour will be restored indicating that you have returned it to the same place.

Highlight Padfile again, click on the Edit menu to reveal the options and click on Copy. Close the floppy window using the button in the right-hand corner of the window and double click on C: drive to open the C: window. Paste the file into this window by clicking on Edit and then Paste. You will see the Padfile appear in the C: window to show you that you have been successful. Close the window using the button in the top right hand corner of the window.

5 Method 2:

Minimise the window marked '3½ Floppy (A:)' by clicking on the left button in the top right-hand corner of the window. Now select C: and then double click on the folder you wish to move or copy to. If the window which is opened occupies the whole screen use the window manipulation buttons in the top right-hand corner of the window to turn the display into a window. Now return the 3½ Floppy window to the screen by clicking on the button with the same name in the toolbar at the bottom of the screen. Again the floppy display should be in a window.

If the windows overlap drag them apart using the mouse pointer until they are completely separate. You can now drag and drop files between the two windows (i.e. between two different folders or drives). Try to drag Padfile from the floppy window into the other window by clicking and holding down the left mouse button and pulling the file into the new window.

Files dragged and dropped from folders in different drives (e.g. A: to C:) are always copied. However, if the folders are both on the same drive (e.g. C:) then the file is moved and not copied. To copy a file in this situation you must hold down the CTRL key on the keyboard when you highlight the file and then drag and drop the file.

6 Explore both methods until you are confident that you can carry out both approaches.

Figure 3.32 Floppy disk

| 1 |
| 2 |
| 3 |
| ✔ 4 |
| 5 |
| 6 |

Word-processing

By the end of this chapter you will be able to:

- create and save a document in a variety of formats;

- open an existing document;

- use the Help function;

- use Insert, Undo, Copy, Move, Paste, Search And Replace functions;

- manipulate text format using different fonts, character sizes, embold, italics, underline, coloured text, alignment options, hypenation, indenting and line spacing;

- format text using tabs, borders, lists and templates;

- complete document using styles, page numbering, spelling and grammatical checking, headers and footers, page orientation and size, and page margins;

- print document including preview and other print options;

- create, manipulate and format a table;

- insert, move, draw and re-size an image;

- use autoshapes;

- import files (i.e. spreadsheets, images, charts) into a document;

- produce and use a mailing list.

The chapter covers Module 2 of the ECDL syllabus. It is divided into tutorials which include exercises that will allow you to practise many of the concepts presented in the text. Each exercise indicates how long it should take you to complete. They can be undertaken anywhere you can gain access to a computer – work, college, a local library, learning centre or at home.

The tutorials in this chapter are as follows:

▷ TUTORIAL 4.1 What is a word-processor?

A word-processor is an application which allows you to create professional documents such as letters, assignments, memoranda and reports. You do not need to be an experienced typist but typing skills are useful. They provide you with a range of functions to allow you to customise documents including fonts (i.e. styles of characters), margins, line spacing, spell checking and tools to import pictures. There are a number of word-processors including Microsoft Word. This is loaded by either double clicking on the Word icon on the desktop or by clicking on Start, selecting Programs and clicking on Microsoft Word. Figure 4.1 shows the application in a window. Your own view may be slightly different since you can change the various toolbars and thus the appearance of the display.

The application (Figure 4.1) consists of three main areas:

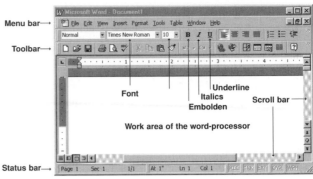

- across the top of the application the title, menu and toolbar which provide you with the design controls for your documents – on first appearance these are complex but it only takes a little practice before they become familiar;

- the work area in which you design documents by entering the text and inserting pictures;

- the status bar across the bottom of the application. Figure 4.1 shows

Figure 4.1 Microsoft Word

Page 1   Sec 1   1/1   At 1"   Ln 1   Col 1

This tells you, you are on page 1, section 1 of your document which consists of a single page (1/1). The rest of the information refers to the position of the cursor of the page. You are entering text at one inch below the top of the page on line 1 in column 1.

A key feature of the application is the toolbars which provide the functions to create, manipulate and format your documents. Many of the options that are provided may be changed when you need to concentrate on different aspects of the process. Figure 4.1 shows the standard and formatting toolbars.

To change a toolbar you need to click on the View menu option which reveals a drop-down menu containing the option Toolbar. If you click on Toolbar, then a list of possible toolbars are provided (Figure 4.2). Figure 4.2 indicates that the standard and formatting toolbar have

Figure 4.2 Toolbar

been selected since a tick is displayed alongside the option. If a toolbar has a tick to the left of it you can remove it by clicking on the tick. This method of changing a toolbar is identical in all Microsoft Office applications.

To add another toolbar, you click on your choice which is either inserted into the toolbar at the top of the application or displayed as a box (Figure 4.3). You can add the free toolbox to the bars by dragging and releasing it over the existing toolbars.

Toolbars can appear complex and formidable but one standard function available in all Microsoft Office application is tooltips. If you rest the mouse pointer on an individual toolbar item, it will cause a small text box to appear,

Figure 4.3 Separate toolbar

giving the title of the option (e.g. Cut, Paste, Print, Zoom etc). This can serve as a useful reminder of the icon's functions.

You may have noticed that some letters of menu and other items (e.g. <u>P</u>rograms) are underlined. Using the keyboard, if you press the letter which is underlined and the Alt key together, it will have the same effect as clicking on the items with the mouse. This is called a keyboard shortcut.

The basics of Microsoft Word

Exercise 4.1

Duration 60 minutes

1 Open Microsoft Word – if the application loads in a window, then use the maximise button in the right-hand corner of the window to expand the application to occupy the full screen.

2 Identify the different functions shown in Figure 4.1 (e.g. work area and menu bar). Explore the different toolbars by inserting and removing new options. When you are familiar with the process of adding and removing them, select only standard and formatting toolbars which are the ones shown in Figure 4.1.

3 When you first load Word, you can create a new document immediately. However, you subsequently need to tell the application that you intend to create a new document. So click on <u>F</u>ile and a drop-down menu will appear with the top item being <u>N</u>ew, but before you click on it read down the menu and notice that it provides functions to <u>S</u>ave, Save <u>A</u>s, <u>P</u>rint and change Page Set<u>u</u>p. The presentation is similar to Wordpad which you used in Chapter 3. Now click on <u>N</u>ew and the New Window appears as shown in Figure 4.5.

4 The New Window provides you with a number of different templates or standard layouts. These are useful in that the layout and presentation has already been decided for particular functions. Explore the different tabs (e.g. General) which, if you click on them, reveal more choices. When you have finished, select the General tab and you should see a template called Blank Document. Choose this template by double clicking on the icon.

5 You are now going to produce your first document. Enter the text below into the work area of the application using the keyboard.

> This is a simple word-processed document based on the blank document template. You create it by entering text using the keyboard.

6 If you make a mistake you can delete a character or word in two different ways using the keyboard. You can use the 'Backspace' key which will delete text to the left while the Delete (sometimes called Del) key will delete text to the right. Figure 4.4 shows the effect of the two keys.

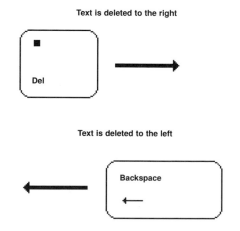

Figure 4.4 Delete keys

7 It is good practice to save your document as soon as you have created it. To save the document,

click on File on the menu bar and a drop-down menu will appear. Click on Save and the Save As window appears. This is identical to Figures 3.26 and 3.27 in Chapter 3 and the procedure for saving a file is the same. Name your file First File and save it on your floppy disk. If you want to update your document then you can overwrite your saved file by clicking on Save again. Try this once you have saved First File and you will notice that no Save As window opens. Microsoft Windows assumes you are saving it to the same location with the same name. If you need to change the location or name you need to use File menu item Save As.

8 You can save files in a variety of formats. The default is normally a Word document. Other formats include:

(a) Document Template

(b) Text (.txt)

(c) Rich Text Format (.rtf)

(c) HTML Document

(d) Works 4.0 for Windows

(f) WordPerfect 5.0

These formats allow the document to be read by other applications. A text or rich text file can be read by most word-processors. A document template allows you to create new templates, HTML is a format suitable for the document to be posted to a website, while Works 4.0 and WordPerfect 5.0 are other word-processor applications. Among the format options are several versions of Microsoft Word. This indicates that different versions of Word use different formats. The normal process is that the latest version of the application will read earlier formats but an old version of Word will be unable to read a new format (e.g. Word 2000 will read all formats but Word 6.0 is unable to read Word 97 or Word 2000.

Practise your file saving by saving your file on to the floppy disk using a variety of formats. Since you have already saved the file once you need to use the File menu Save As option. The Save As (Figure 4.6) window will appear and if you click on the black triangle button next to Save as type box, then a drop-down list will appear of alternative formats. You select the new format by double clicking on it. A black triangle button always indicates a menu or list of other options.

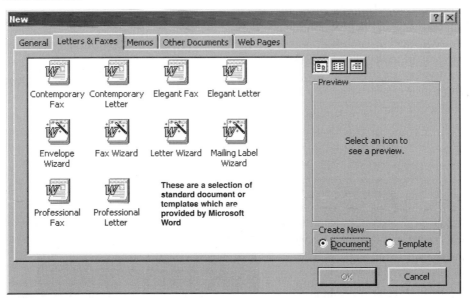

Figure 4.5 New Window

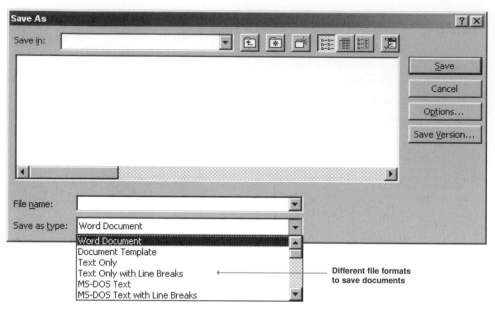

Different file formats
to save documents

Figure 4.6 Saving in different file formats

Change the file name by adding a number (e.g. First File 2 etc.) and formats to Text, Rich Text Format, WordPerfect 5.0, Word 6.0/95, HTML and Document Template in turn. You may be presented with messages telling you that you may lose data by saving in this format but ignore them. Netherless, in practice, by making a file readable for other applications you may change its presentation.

On the <u>F</u>ile menu is an option Save as <u>H</u>TML which allows you to save the document in a format suitable for posting to a website. This is an alternative way of saving your file in this format rather than the standard Save <u>A</u>s option.

When you are saving each new format to your floppy disk you will notice that not all the files appear. This is because the system only looks for files that match your chosen format. The others are essentially invisible to the application. If you view the floppy disk by accessing it through the My Computer icon on the desktop, you will be able to see all the files you have saved. Figure 4.7 illustrates what your floppy may contain. The files vary in size and some have new descriptions.

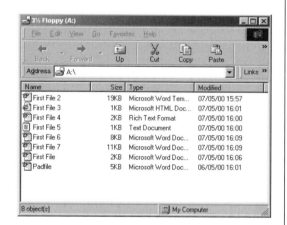

Figure 4.7 Files on the floppy disk

9 You can change the appearance of the display using the zoom tool which is provided on the Standard toolbar and as the last item on the <u>V</u>iew menu. Figure 4.8 shows zoom on the toolbar. You can change the display by clicking on any of the list of options.

Figure 4.8 Zoom

Explore a few options and see which you prefer.

10 You can now close your document by clicking on File and a drop-down menu will reveal an option called Close. Click on Close and the working area will be cleared. If you have made a change to your document since you last saved it then you will be prompted to save the amended document.

TUTORIAL 4.2   Help function

All Microsoft Office applications provide an identical Help function. It is accessed and used in the same way so by understanding how to use Help in Microsoft Word you will be able to use the function in all applications. The Help function is located on the menu bar of the applications. If you click on the Help menu item then a display similar to Figure 4.9 will appear. If you click on the Contents and Index option, you will be presented with a list of the contents of the Help function. You can search the list by entering a word in the top box.

Figure 4.9 Word Help menu

Figure 4.10 shows the results of a search to locate items related to grammar checking your

document. If your query is contained in the Help function, then you can display the item by clicking on the Display button. You will often find that your search reveals several items linked to your word. In the grammar example there are five. To access the help information, simply highlight the option of your choice and double click on the Display button. Figure 4.11 shows the result of Displaying grammar checking. A window of sub-options appears. You can select any option by highlighting and clicking on the Display button. This will reveal the actual help (Figure 4.12).

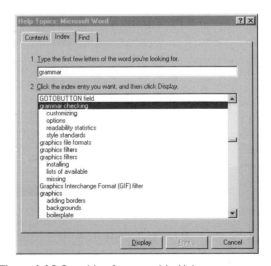

Figure 4.10 Searching for a word in Help

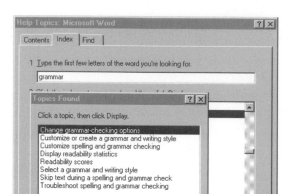

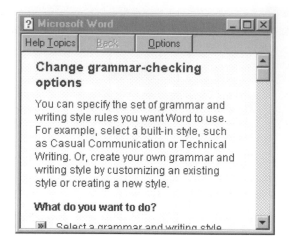

Figure 4.12 Help text

Figure 4.11 Extra options in searching for a word in Help

▶ **Help**   **Duration 30 minutes**

Exercise 4.2

1 Using the method to access Help described in Tutorial 4.2, search for Help about locating help. Click on the Help menu item, then Contents and Index. Enter help and double click on the option, 'locating' and a Topics Found window will appear with two options. Select by double clicking on the option 'Ways to get assistance while you work'.

The Help tutorial will appear as shown in Figure 4.13.

2 Each of the boxes with a red bar provides a brief tutorial about different aspects of Help. Click on each to access the tutorial. Work your way through the material to gain an insight into Help.

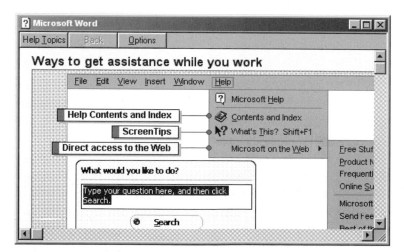

Figure 4.13 Help tutorial

TUTORIAL 4.3   Creating a complex document

Microsoft Word is a professional word-processor that can be used to produce a wide range of documents from a single paragraph note to a report with scores of pages. When you first start it, the work area will be blank except for the flashing cursor. The cursor shows the start of the first line of the new document. Word will automatically give your document a name which you can see on the title line above the menu. It is likely that it has been called Document 1. You can change this name later when you save the file.

In order to understand the process of developing a high-quality document, you need to enter a lot of text which may seem a tiresome process but it is very important to experience the nature of the word-processor. In many ways, it does not matter how poorly the text is entered since you have access to tools to change its appearance, layout and structure.

 Entering text

Duration 45 minutes

Exercise 4.3

1 Enter the passage below. There is no need to break the text into paragraphs and do not be concerned if you make any errors. You can format the passage and correct errors later.

The postcard has been used in Great Britain for more than a hundred years. In 1896 the Post Office officially allowed picture postcards to be sent through the post. Plain cards had been permitted for several years but the new development caught the imagination of the population so that within a few years, hundreds of millions of postcards were being sent. The role of the postcard in communications was broadly similar to modern usage in that people sent many cards when they were away on holiday. However, cards were also used in place of a telephone which few people had access to, so many cards contained messages about business (e.g. ordering goods), arranging meetings between friends and sending greetings (e.g. birthdays, Christmas and New Year). The speed of delivery was very fast with the possibility of post arriving the same day. Picture postcards were available at the start of the century on many themes. This included many subjects which still occur on modern cards such as comic, seaside views, artistic and street scenes. They also included many themes and subjects which are now rare such as recording disasters (e.g. fires and floods). Many Edwardian and Victorian families collected an album of cards rather like people now have a photograhic collections. These albums have become the modern source of many collectable cards, having spent 90 years in people's lofts. Before the First World War the desire to collect postcards was very widespread and millions of cards ended their days in an album. The First World War brought about many changes both to the content and availability of cards. Many were produced documenting the nature of the war showing shell and zeppelin raid damage and aimed at raising funds for the war effort. However, at the same time paper was in short supply so that the quality and quantity of some postcards were reduced. These changes contributed to a reduced interest in postcards which continued to fall during the 1920s until few people collected cards by the Second World War. In the 1960s the concept of collecting cards returned but rather than being a collection of cards sent to you, they were based on people collecting a particular theme such as cards of your home town, by a particular artist or a special subject. Interest grew rapidly during the next thirty years until there are now thousands of postcard collectors in Great Britain. Postcard collecting is now a worldwide hobby.

2 Save the passage on your floppy disk under the file name Postcard.

3 Close your file using the close option on the File menu or using the Close button in the right hand corner of the window. However, you will notice that there are two sets of buttons because two windows are open. The first contains Word and the second your document. You need to close the document window, which is the lower set of buttons.

4 Once you have saved and closed your file, your document window will be blanked so you must either start a new document or open an existing document. We have already discussed starting a new document so let us consider opening an existing document.

5 Click on File and a drop-down menu will appear with a list of options. Among them will be Open. Click on Open and the Open window shown in Figure 4.14 will appear. You need to select where your file is located (i.e. disk and folder) by using the black triangle button next to the Look in box which reveals a list of options, similar to the Save As window. Select Floppy Disk and you will see a list of files that are stored on the disk appears in the work area. The File of type box should read, 'All Files'. If any other message appears, then the only file corresponding to that format will be shown, so change the entry to All Files if Postcard is not visible. You open Postcard either by highlighting the entry in the work area and clicking on the Open button or by double clicking the Postcard entry.

6 The document will be displayed in Word. You can open more than one file at a time and they will load one after another so that you only see the latest document but all the others are still there. It is rather like a pile of papers, where you can only see the top one. If you have other documents on your floppy disk, then open another one now. This document will appear in Word and hide Postcard. To see Postcard you need to close the top document using either the window close button or the Close option in the File menu.

7 Close Postcard and Microsoft Word by using the window close button in the top right-hand corner or use the Exit option in the File menu.

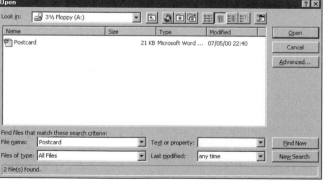

Figure 4.14 Opening a file

TUTORIAL 4.4 Manipulating text

Microsoft Word and other modern word-processors provide you with many functions to manipulate your documents. They allow you to:

- ✒ insert paragraphs;
- ✒ insert page breaks;
- ✒ add headings;
- ✒ change the font of all or part of your document;
- ✒ change the size of the font for all or part of your document.

These are powerful aids to the presentation of your text. In addition word-processors provide tools to copy chunks of text from one place to another. These are available on the Standard toolbar and on the Edit menu (see Figure 4.15). You can choose which set of functions to use. There are three – Cut, Copy and Paste. The process is to highlight the text you wish to work on and then click on Copy or Cut. Copy leaves the original text untouched while Cut removes the chosen text. Move the cursor to the new position and select the Paste function. This places the text in its new position. When you Copy or Cut text, it is stored in a temporary location called the Clipboard. The Clipboard can only hold one item at a time therefore you must complete the cycle of Cut or Copy and Paste each time for each item before repeating the process.

Cut, Copy and Paste can be used to move information between, as well as within, Microsoft Office applications (e.g. Microsoft Excel to Word). The functions try to copy information in a form which the importing application can edit. Thus Excel data is transferred as a Word table. If this is not possible then selected information is pasted as an embedded object which can be edited by the originating application. If this in turn is not possible, the information is inserted as a static image which cannot be edited. On the Edit menu, an extra function is provided called Paste Special which provides some control over the format of the pasted object.

The Standard toolbar provides an additional function called the Format Painter (see Figure 4.15). If you click on the Format Painter icon your mouse pointer changes shape to a paint brush. If you drag the pointer over an area of text, you copy the area's format (e.g. font, character size etc.). This can be painted on to another area by clicking on Format Painter again and dragging the brush pointer over another area.

The Edit menu provides useful functions to locate and change particular words and phrases within a document (Figure 4.16). This is very useful in long documents. Simply type the word or phrase you are seeking into the Find what box and the replacement in the Replace with box. The option is enacted by clicking on Find Next button. The document is searched and as each match is made, you are given the choice of making the change or moving to the next match.

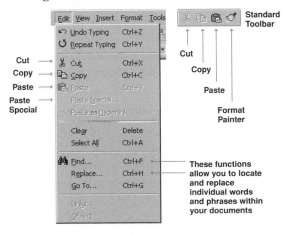

Figure 4.15 Copy, Cut and Paste

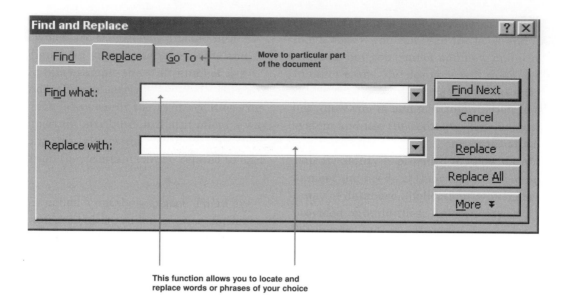

Find and Replace

Find | Replace | Go To ← Move to particular part of the document

Find what: [   ] ▼   Find Next

Cancel

Replace with: [   ] ▼   Replace

Replace All

More ⬇

This function allows you to locate and replace words or phrases of your choice

Figure 4.16 Find and Replace

Editing a document

Duration 60 minutes

1 Load Microsoft Word.

2 Open Postcard file.

3 The Postcard document is essentially a large block of text without any basic structure, so our first task is to break it into a series of paragraphs. This is a straightforward task. You first need to select the place to insert a new paragraph. Position the mouse pointer over the spot and click to move the cursor in the new position. (This is a general method of moving the cursor to insert a paragraph, page break, a word, a sentence or a chunk of text.) By pressing enter twice a new paragraph is created. The first enter moves the text at the right of the cursor to a new line, and the second enter separates the text with a blank line.

4 Divide the document into five paragraphs:

End of first paragraph

a few years, hundreds of millions of postcards were being sent.

Start of second paragraph

The role of the postcard in communications was broadly

End of second paragraph

The speed of delivery was very fast with the possibility of post arriving the same day.

Start of third paragraph

Picture postcards were available at the start of the century on many themes.

End of third paragraph

and millions of cards ended their days in an album.

Start of fourth paragraph

The First World War brought about
many changes

End of fourth paragraph

until few people collected cards by the
Second World War.

Start of fifth paragraph

In the 1960s the concept of collecting
cards

Observe what happens after each press of the
enter key. At the end of the process, Postcard
should now be divided into five paragraphs.

5 In addition to dividing a document into
paragraphs, you can also insert page breaks. The
first step is to position your mouse pointer over
the place you intend to insert the page break and
click the mouse button to move the cursor in the
new position. Click on Insert which opens a drop-
down menu with the option Break. Click on Break
to open the Break window shown in Figure 4.17.
This window provides a variety of options but the
default is to insert a page break. So simply click
on the OK button.

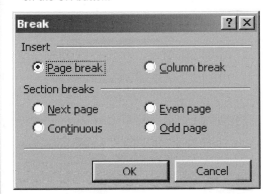

Figure 4.17 Page breaks

6 Insert a page break at the start of the second
paragraph.

7 Postcard is now a two-page document with the
first page consisting of a single paragraph which

is probably not very suitable. How can we reverse
this mistake? All Microsoft Office applications
contain a function to reverse an action. This is
called Undo and in case you undo something by
accident, there is also a redo function. Undo can
reverse a series of actions, so it can be very
useful.

8 To undo the page break, you can either click on
the undo icon on the toolbar or select the Undo
option on the Edit menu. Use one method to
remove the page break and then replace it using
the redo icon or Redo. Practise the process until
you are confident about using Undo and Redo.

9 A word-processed document is essentially never
finished because you can always add extra words,
change the layout and manipulate the document.
This allows you to continuously develop a piece of
writing. The Postcard document needs a title to
introduce it. To insert a heading at the start of the
document, you first need to provide sufficient
space for the title. Place the cursor at the start of
the document in front of the word, 'The Postcard',
and press enter three times. This will add three
blank lines to the start of the document. Use the
arrow keys to move the cursor up two lines and
enter 'Postcard Collecting'. The top of your
document should now read:

Postcard Collecting

The postcard has been used in Great
Britain for more than a hundred years.
In 1896, the Post Office officially
allowed picture postcards to be sent
through the post.

10 We now need to emphasise this title. In order for
Word functions to act on text you need to select
or highlight it. To do this, position the mouse
pointer at the start of the text (in this case before
the P in Postcard) and holding the left mouse
button down, move the pointer to the end of
Collecting and release the button. Postcard
Collecting will be highlighted.

11 With the text highlighted you can now change the font and size of characters to make the heading stand out. On the Formatting toolbar you have access to the functions which control the choice of font and font size. Figure 4.18 shows this part of the toolbar.

12 Click on the small button with the down-pointing black triangle next to the font box. A drop-down list of different fonts appears. The list is scrollable, so you can use the scroll bars to explore it. To select a new font, double click on a font and the heading will immediately change. It still remains highlighted so explore the fonts until you find one that you like in order so as to practise the technique. When you are satisfied, simply click away from the highlighted area to remove it and make the change.

13 Now repeat the process for the size box. Select the small black triangle button to reveal a list of sizes. Experiment with different sizes until you find a suitable size.

14 You have been working on two words. Now highlight the whole passage except for the title. Position mouse pointer before the first word of the document (i.e. The Postcard) and hold down the left mouse button and move it to the end of the passage (i.e. 'a worldwide hobby') and release the button. The whole passage should now be highlighted. People often find this needs practice so keep trying if you do not succeed the first time.

Change the font and character size of the whole document.

15 You have now selected two words and the whole text. Using the same technique you can highlight and act on a single character, a word, a sentence or a paragraph as well. Practise highlighting different numbers of characters, words and paragraphs until you are confident of your ability to highlight text.

16 Select a sentence within the document and copy it to the end of the document. You do this by first highlighting the sentence, then click on Edit and a drop-down menu will appear. Select Copy by clicking on it. Now move the cursor to the end of the document and click on the Paste option with the Edit menu. You will see your copied text appear. Now highlight this new sentence and move it again using the Cut function. Again once the sentence is highlighted. Click on Edit and then Cut. The sentence will disappear. Move the cursor to the beginning of the document and Paste it in. A new sentence will now begin your document. You can remove this new sentence which is now in the wrong place by highlighting it and pressing the delete key.

17 Repeat this process of cutting, copying and pasting until you are confident of the process but leave your document unchanged.

18 Save your document as a file called New Postcard and close Word.

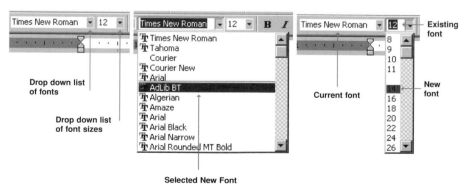

Figure 4.18 Font and font size functions

TUTORIAL 4.5 Formatting toolbar and menu

The Formatting toolbar contains a number of tools which are very useful to format a document. These are:

✍ embolding, italics and underlining;

✍ justification—left, centred, right and double;

✍ highlighting text;

✍ font colour.

Figure 4.19 shows these functions. The bold, italics and underlining functions are switched on by clicking on their icons as illustrated in Figure 4.19. With the function selected, the text entered is in the chosen characteristic (e.g. **Bold,** *italics* and <u>underlined</u>*).

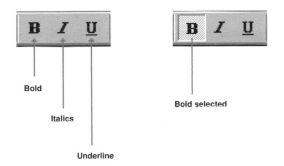

Figure 4.19 Bold, Italics and Underlining

The highlighting function allows you to select a colour from a palette which is accessed by clicking on the down button next to the Pen icon (see Figure 4.20). Once you have selected a colour, you highlight your chosen text by clicking on the icon, which changes the pointer to resemble a highlight pen. You drag this pen over the text by holding down the left mouse button at the start of the text and then release the button at the end of the text (e.g Highlight).

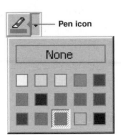

Figure 4.20 Highlighting

The font colour operates by providing you with a choice of colours which is revealed by clicking on the down button next to the icon (see Figure 4.21). Once you have selected a colour you can create the coloured text by simply typing the words which will then appear in the chosen colour. The bar of the font colour icon shows your choice.

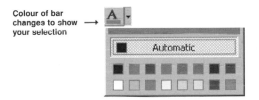

Figure 4.21 Font Colour

The overall appearance of a document is influenced by the justification (Figure 4.22) of the text. There are four options:

✍ Left – the left text edge is parallel with the margin and the right is ragged.

✍ Right – the right text edge is parallel with the margin and the left is ragged.

✍ Centred – text is aligned down the centre of the page with both edges ragged.

✍ Full – both left and right text edges are parallel with the margins.

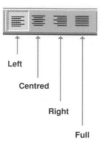

Figure 4.22 Justification

The <u>P</u>aragraph window (Figure 4.25) allows you to indent your text, change line spacing and change the tabs for the document. This controls the distance of each tab (i.e. the distance of an indent produced by pressing the tab key).

In addition to the options available on the Format toolbar, there is also a F<u>o</u>rmat menu (Figure 4.23) which duplicates many of these functions but also provides new possibilities. The Paragraph option (Figure 4.24) provides a variety of formatting functions. The menu also provides for producing bullet pointed and numbered lists (i.e. Bullets and <u>N</u>umbering option). A wide range of different bullet points are offered.

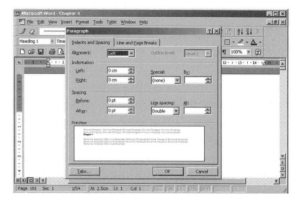

Figure 4.24 Paragraph option

Figure 4.23 F<u>o</u>rmat menu

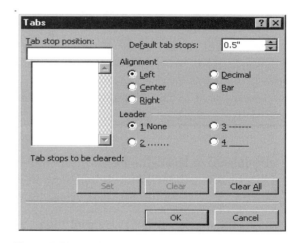

Figure 4.25 Tab function

▶ Format a document

Duration 30 minutes

Exercise 4.5

1 Load Microsoft Word.

2 Open the New Postcard file.

3 Highlight the whole document and explore the

different options within the toolbar and Paragraph options in the following ways:

(a) Change the line spacing to 1.5, 2.0, 2.5 and 3.0 and select which one you prefer.

(b) Change the justification of the document from left, right, centred and full.

(c) Change the colour of the font using the toolbar option until you find the colour you prefer.

4. Highlight the first sentence of the document and explore the different options within the toolbar and Paragraph options in the following ways:

(a) Use the bold, italics and underline options to emphasise the whole sentence, individual or groups of words. Systematically use all three options.

(b) Use the colour highlighting option on the whole sentence, individual and group of words. Explore the different possibilities. This method is often used to emphasise a phrase or word or to show where you have made changes to a document.

(c) Change the tabs and explore their use on the document.

5. Once you are content that you understand this wide range of functions then save your document if you want to preserve your work and close Word.

▶ TUTORIAL 4.6 Templates, page format, styles, headers and footers, spelling and grammar checking

Word provides you with many different ways of presenting a document. You can select standard layouts which are called templates or styles for documents such as letters, memos, CVs and website designs. You can create your own templates or simply specify the margins for all four paper edges, the orientation (i.e. portrait or landscape) and the size of paper.

In the File menu is an option called Page Setup which is shown in Figure 4.26. This allows you to change the size of all four margins, and the header and footer. The preview area lets you to see what the page will look like. The Page Setup window has tabs that allow you to choose the orientation and size of the paper. You can make these selections at any time. It is not necessary to make your decisions before you start. At any time during or after you have written the document, you can modify the layout.

Figure 4.27 illustrates the four margins you are able to set with Word. They are all

individual so it is possible to have all four different. In addition to a top and bottom margin, you can set headers and footers (see Figure 4.28). These are areas of the page where you can present standard messages that appear on every page such as a title as a header and a copyright statement as a footer. These overlap with each other.

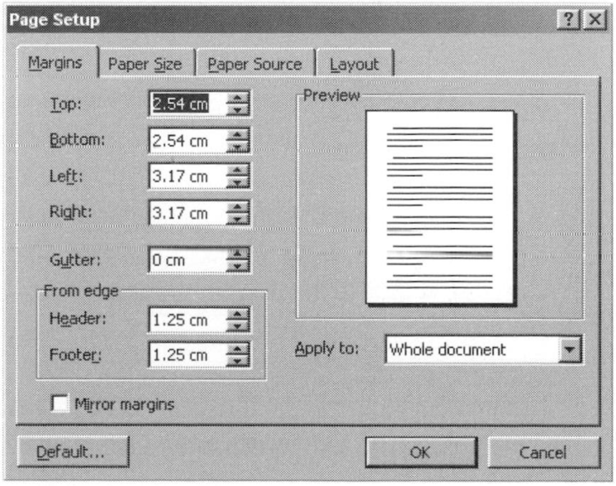

Figure 4.26 Page Setup

To insert a header or footer message you must click on <u>V</u>iew and a drop-down menu will appear with the option <u>H</u>eader and Footer. If you click on this option then a outline box will appear with a toolbox (Figure 4.29). This allows you to create the header message. When you have finished you can move to footer by simply pressing the down arrow and a footer outline will appear. You do not have to have a pair. You are free to have only a header or a footer. As with all other features of the Word document you can change your text later. The header and footer appear in a lighter colour to other text at the top and bottom of the page, respectively.

Figure 4.29 Headers and footers

These features are essentially about creating a high-quality document by providing a framework or structure for the text to reside in. There are two other functions which are concerned with quality but focus on the text. These are the spelling and grammar checker. You can use these functions (see Figure 4.30) to check your writing at any time you choose. The check will begin from any point in the document where your cursor is positioned and will continue until the whole document is covered or you choose to stop. You select the checkers by clicking on <u>T</u>ools and a drop-down menu appears with the option <u>S</u>pelling and Grammar. If you click on this option, the checkers start and the Spelling and Grammar window appears every time the function detects a possible spelling or grammatical error. The function allows you to choose between options (i.e. alternative spellings or grammatical changes) or to decide your original words are correct. It is important to realise that the function only identifies potential mistakes.

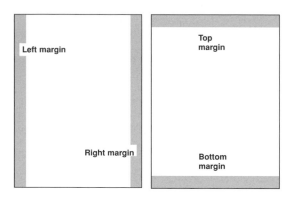

Figure 4.27 Margins

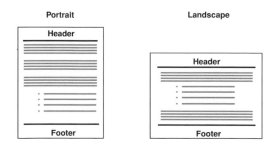

Figure 4.28 Presentation of headers and footers

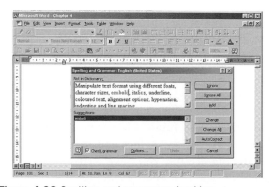

Figure 4.30 Spelling and grammar checking

Templates

Duration 45 minutes

1 Open Word and begin a new document by clicking on <u>F</u>ile and the <u>N</u>ew option. The New window will appear with a selection of templates to chose from. Select the Letters & Fax tab and double click on Contemporary Letter. The template will appear (Figure 4.31).

2 Enter the information below into the template:

Return Address   Recipient's Address

Anywhere Staff Agency   Ms Janet Spenser
23 Any Street   Specialist Fabric
Anytown   Designers
Anyshire   345 New Anything Road
AN12 5YT   Anytown
                        AN24 8UY

Dear Ms Spenser,

Thank you for your enquiry concerning the availability of temporary office staff . We have several people on our register which would meet your requirements. I have attached their details for your assessment and they are all available for interview during the next two weeks. If you would like to interview any of our temps please contact me and I will make the arrangements.

Yours sincerely,

J.W. Anderson
Personnel Manager

3 Once you have created the letter you should spell and grammar check it by clicking on the <u>T</u>ools menu item and then <u>S</u>pelling and Grammar. This will launch the checker shown in Figure 4.30. You will notice that it starts to check the letter from the position of your cursor but will continue until you have completed the whole document or until you choose to stop. The checker allows you to decide whether or not to accept its options for changes to spelling or grammar.

4 Experiment with the page layout by clicking on <u>F</u>ile and then Page Set<u>u</u>p and explore changing the four margins, the orientation of page (e.g. landscape and portrait) and paper size. The options are available under the different tabs (e.g. <u>M</u>argins and Paper <u>S</u>ize).

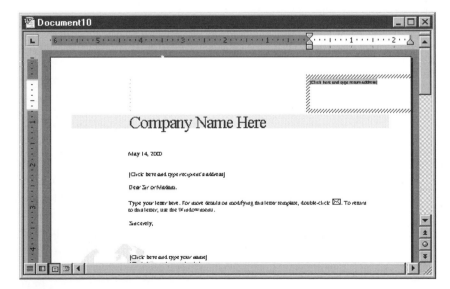

Figure 4.31 Contemporary Letter template

5 Insert a header and footer to the letter. Click on View and then option Header and Footer. Explore the toolbar and experiment with the different options but create a header, 'Anywhere Staff Agency' and a footer, 'Confidential' and the date.

6 Once you have completed your letter then print it by clicking on File and the Print Preview which allows you to see what your document will look like once it is printed. If you are satisfied with the letter then print it by closing Print Preview using the Close button on the toolbar (Figure 4.32) and click on File, Print option and OK button.

Figure 4.32 Print Preview

▶ **TUTORIAL 4.7   Tables, pictures and importing objects**

A key function of modern word-processors is their ability to present information in the form of a table. Microsoft Word provides a range of options for creating and amending tables. These allow you to both insert and remove rows and columns, as well as adjust the size of cells, although Word will automatically format the table for you. All the table options are available through the Table menu and on the Standard toolbar. Figure 4.33 illustrates the Table menu and Figure 4.34 the toolbar icons.

The Table menu shows a range of options for customising your tables. By clicking on the Insert Table you can place a table into your documents at the cursor's position. When you select Insert Table, you are prompted by the application for the number of rows and columns which your table will contain. Word will automatically calculate the size of columns and rows which will fit the required table on to the page. It is not vital that you know the exact number of rows and columns since you can later adjust the table by adding or removing them.

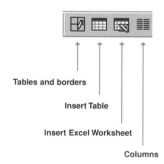

Figure 4.34 Toolbar table icons

In addition to placing a table in your documents you can also insert pictures (e.g. clipart), the products of other applications which are called objects in Word (e.g. Excel spreadsheets), page numbers and even extra pages. These functions allow you to produce high-quality documents. Figure 4.35 illustrates where the picture, object, page numbers and pages functions are located.

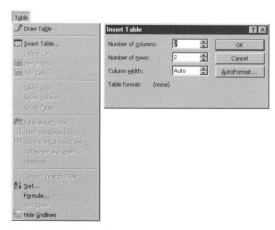

Figure 4.33 Table menu

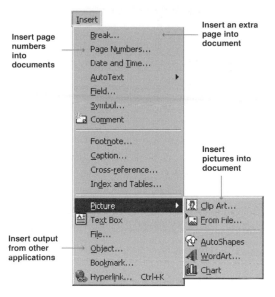

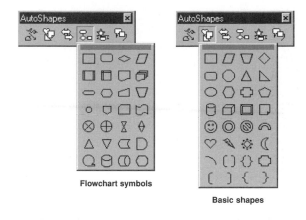

Flowchart symbols

Basic shapes

Figure 4.36 AutoShapes

Figure 4.35 Pictures

There is another way to add drawings to your documents. This is available from the Drawing toolbar and the Insert menu as part of the Picture sub-menu in the AutoShapes option. AutoShapes provide you with many standard shapes (e.g. lines, basic shapes, arrows, flowchart symbols, stars and banners and callouts – speech balloons). Figure 4.36 shows some AutoShapes.

Tables   **Duration 60 minutes**

Exercise 4.7

1 Open Word and begin a new document by clicking on File and the New option. The New window will appear with a selection of templates to choose from. Select Blank Document by double clicking on icon.

2 Create a table to include the following information:

Item	Age (cms)	Height (kgms)	Weight
John	23	156	70
Anne	34	135	50
Janet	19	141	61
Perry	42	150	72

Click on Table menu item, Insert Table, select 4 columns and 5 rows and then click OK button.

3 Insert a blank column between Item and Age and a blank row between each of the rows using functions in Table menu. To insert a column, you must initially select it by placing the cursor in your selected column and clicking on Select Column. A new function appears in the menu called Insert Column which allows you to insert a new column in relation to the select column. The new column appears to the left of the selected column.

4 To insert a new row, you must again select a row but simply placing your cursor in the row is sufficient so that the Insert Row function appears.

By clicking on this function, this will insert a new row above the select row.

5 To remove rows and columns, you must initially select them and then choose <u>D</u>elete Rows or <u>D</u>elete Columns and in this case to select a row involves you in using the Select <u>R</u>ow option. Practise inserting and deleting rows and columns until you are confident that you can carry out the task.

6 You will have noticed that, like other Word functions which require you to highlight the area you want to operate on, you need to select areas of the table to work on.

7 Select the whole table by clicking on <u>T</u>able menu and then Select T<u>a</u>ble option. The whole table will be highlighted. You can now change the size of the individual table cells by selecting the Cell Height and <u>W</u>idth options. When you click on this option a window (Figure 4.37) appears. This allows you change the height of the rows and width of the columns. By selecting individual rows or columns, you can change the height and width of the individual row or column.

8 Experiment with changing the characteristics of the whole table and then those of the individual rows and columns until you are confident that you can carry out the tasks. It is also possible to add different borders to the table using the Format menu or Outside border option on the toolbar. This involves highlighting the whole table and then selecting the option from the menu (i.e. <u>B</u>orders and Shading) or toolbar. Explore the different borders and select the one you prefer.

9 Insert a picture after your table by clicking on the <u>I</u>nsert menu item and then <u>P</u>icture which will reveal the sub-menu shown in Figure 4.35. Click on <u>C</u>lip Art which will open the Microsoft Clip Gallery (Figure 4.38). This is a library of clip art and pictures from which you can select images to insert in your documents. You select an image by clicking on it (it is then surrounded by a box) and then clicking <u>I</u>nsert. The clip art or picture is inserted into your document where your cursor is placed.

10 Insert a picture or clip art image of your choice. You can manipulate the image when it is placed in your document by single clicking on the image which will be enclosed by a box. This is shown in Figure 4.38. If you place your mouse pointer over one of the small black squares the pointer will become double-headed and you can drag the image around – making it larger or smaller. Practise changing the size of the image. You can also align the image (i.e. left, right and centre the image) using the tools on the Formatting toolbar.

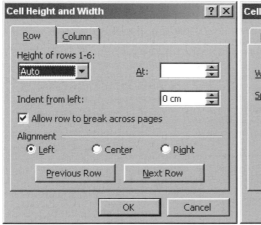
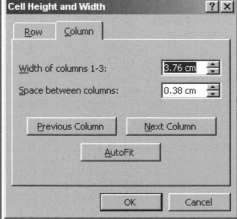

Figure 4.37 Adjusting cell height and width

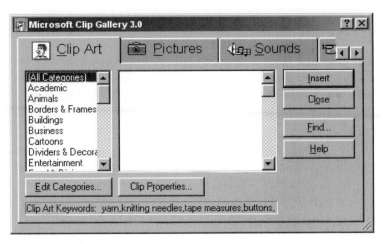

Figure 4.38 Microsoft Clip Gallery

11 Place your mouse pointer between the table and the image and click on Insert and then Break. This will reveal the Break window (Figure 4.39) which allows you to insert a page break between the table and the image by clicking on OK. This is a simple but very useful function in that it allows you to adjust the layout of the document.

12 Your document is now at least two pages long so we can number the pages by using the Page Numbers option in the Insert menu. When you click on this option a Page Numbers window appears (Figure 4.40) which allows you to customise the position, alignment and format of numbers. Explore the options and number the pages of your document.

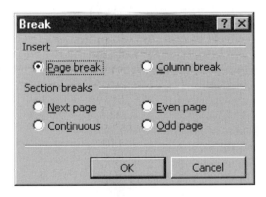

Figure 4.39 Page break

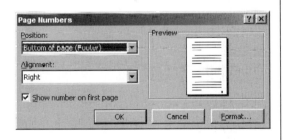

Figure 4.40 Page Numbers

13 Save your document and close Word.

> ## ▶ TUTORIAL 4.8 Mail merging

Mail merging can help you produce individualised letters, envelopes and other documents without the need to adjust and change each one. A major use of mail merging is to produce a standard letter but with names and addresses added from a list. This allows high-quality personalised letters to be produced. You need to create two types of document – a main document (i.e. the standard letter) and a data source (i.e. a list of names and addresses). Mail merge allows you to link the two to produce individualised documents.

In Word, mail merge is available within the Tools menu and Mail Merge option. Figure 4.41 shows you the Mail Merge Helper which is opened when you click on the option. This assists you to produce a main document, a data source and then combine the two together so that you can produce a personalised result. Your main document can be new or an existing one and so can your data source. By clicking on Create or Get Data buttons you are guided through the steps you need to take to undertake a mail merge. You must initially produce a main document before you are allowed to link to an existing data source or create a new data source.

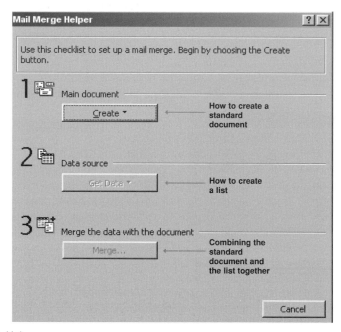

Figure 4.41 Mail Merge Helper

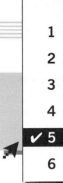

| 1 |
| 2 |
| 3 |
| 4 |
| ✔ 5 |
| 6 |

Spreadsheets

By the end of this chapter you should understand how to:

- create and save a spreadsheet in a variety of formats;

- open and close an existing spreadsheet;

- use the Help function;

- change view mode and use zoom tool;

- modify a toolbar;

- enter numbers, text, symbols and simple formulas into a cell;

- use Undo, Copy, Move, Paste, Delete, Search and Replace functions;

- insert rows and columns;

- sort data;

- use formulas and functions;

- format cells for numbers, text and cell ranges;

- set up a document using margins, headers and footers, and page orientation and size;

- print a spreadsheet using basic options including preview;

- import files (i.e. word, images, charts etc.) into a spreadsheet;

- move and resize imported objects;

- use charts and graphs.

The chapter covers Module 3 of the ECDL syllabus. It is divided into six tutorials which include exercises that will allow you to practise many of the ideas presented in the text. Each exercise indicates how long it should take you to complete. They can be undertaken anywhere you can gain access to a computer – work, college, a local library or at home.

The tutorials covered in this chapter are as follows:

▶ TUTORIAL 5.1 What is a spreadsheet?

Spreadsheets were one of the major applications that originally established the personal computer. They are applications that aim to exploit the computer's power to manipulate numbers. Spreadsheets allow you to develop numerical models of almost any transaction which uses numbers (e.g. profit and loss accounts). In addition they are extremely useful when you need to present information in the form of a table. In this case they can present text as well as numbers.

Spreadsheets are used extensively in business, government, research and education for a wide range of purposes. These include:

- profit and loss accounts;

- project plans;

- experimental data;

- model processes.

Microsoft Excel is illustrated in Figure 5.1. The application has three main areas. These are the menu and toolbars, work area and status bar. The menu and toolbar areas are very similar to other Microsoft Office applications (e.g. Word) and operate in exactly the same way. You should notice that there is an additional line called the formula bar. This indicates which cell is currently active and if there is a formula in that cell. The work area is quite distinctive in that it is divided into a grid of rows and columns. The columns are each labelled with a letter and rows with a number so that each cell has a unique title (e.g. E11 – column and row). The status line shows which worksheet you are working on and that it is ready for input. You can work on multiple worksheets.

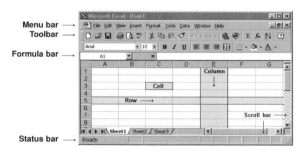

Menu bar →
Toolbar →

Formula bar →

Status bar →

Figure 5.1 Microsoft Excel

Key features of the application are the toolbars which provide the functions to create and manipulate your worksheets. You have access to a number of different toolbars which provide many different functions. Figure 5.2 shows the standard and formatting toolbars. Compare these toolbars with those provided by Word. There are many similarities and some important differences. To use these different functions requires you to change the toolbars.

To change a toolbar click on the <u>V</u>iew menu option which reveals a drop-down menu containing the option <u>T</u>oolbar. If you click on <u>T</u>oolbar then a list of possible toolbars are provided. Those which have been selected are indicated by having a tick alongside their names. A toolbar can be removed by clicking on the option and the tick and toolbar will be removed. To add a new toolbar simply click on the one you need. A tick appears alongside and it is made available. This method of changing the toolbar is identical to all Microsoft Office applications (see Chapter 4). The new toolbar is either inserted into the toolbars at the top of the application or displayed as a box. You can add the free toolbox to the bars by dragging and releasing it over the existing toolbars.

All Microsoft Office applications provide an identical <u>H</u>elp function. It is accessed and used in the same way in all applications and was explained in Tutorial 4.2 in Chapter 4. The <u>H</u>elp function is located on the menu bar of

Standard
toolbar

Formula
toolbar

Figure 5.2 Standard and Formula toolbars

Excel. If you click on the Help menu item then Figure 5.3 will appear. If you click on the Contents and Index option you will be presented with a list of the contents of the Help function. You can search the list by entering a word in the top box.

Figure 5.3 Microsoft Excel Help menu

The basics of Microsoft Excel

Duration 60 minutes

Exercise 5.1

1 Load Microsoft Excel either by double clicking on the Excel icon on the Desktop or by clicking on Start, selecting Programs and then Microsoft Excel. Figure 5.1 shows the spreadsheet application in a window. If your computer displays the application in a window, expand it to fill the screen by using the maximise button in the top right-hand corner of the window.

2 Figure 5.4 illustrates Excel with the standard and formatting toolbars. Explore the toolbars using the View menu and then select the Toolbar option to reveal the different toolbars. Select and remove toolbars until you are confident about the process and stop with the standard and formatting toolbars selected. You can select a new toolbar by clicking on it. A selected toolbar is shown by a tick being displayed alongside its name.

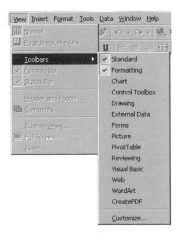

Figure 5.4 Toolbars options in View menu

3 Excel loads ready to create a new spreadsheet worksheet. You will notice on the title bar that a name Book1 has already been provided. This name can be changed when you save the sheet. If you click on one of the cells in the work area, you will see it highlighted. You can move around the work area by using the mouse pointer to select a cell or by using the arrow keys on the keyboard. Practise moving around the sheet. You will see that the title of each individual cell (e.g. C9) will appear on the left of the formula bar.

4 Excel provides you with a range of templates. The application opens with the basic Worksheet template in a similar way that Word provides you with the Blank Document template. They are available to you through the File menu and then you select New to open the New window. Explore what is available to you.

5 Enter the information shown in Figure 5.5 to create your first spreadsheet. If you make a mistake you can click on the cell again and simply re-enter your information. The new information will overwrite the original entry. Alternatively you can use the Undo function. This will remove the last action you have performed. You can Undo a series of actions. If you Undo one too many a Redo function is also provided. Practise using these functions as they are very useful. They are available in the Edit menu (Figure 5.6) and on the Standard toolbar (Figure 5.6).

Figure 5.5 Exercise

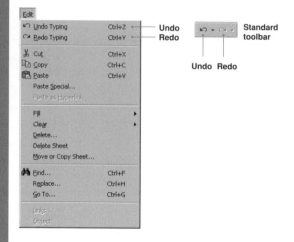

Figure 5.6 Undo and Redo

6 It is good practice to save your spreadsheet as soon as you have created it. To save the sheet, click on File on the menu bar and a drop-down menu will appear. Click on Save and the Save As window appears. This is identical to Figure 3.25 in Chapter 3 and the procedure for saving a file is the same. Name your file First Sheet and save it on your floppy disk. You may hear your floppy disk save the sheet. If you want to update your document then you can overwrite your saved file by clicking on Save again. Try this once you have saved First Sheet and you will notice that no Save As window opens. Microsoft Windows assumes you are saving it to the same location with the same name. If you need to change location or name you need to use File menu item Save As.

7 Figure 5.7 illustrates the Save As window with some of the different formats that spreadsheets can be saved in. The standard for Excel is Microsoft Excel Workbook. Saving the file in different formats allows you to load it into other spreadsheet applications. There are several versions of Excel which are designated by a number (e.g. Excel 5.0). The latest version will read all the files produced by earlier versions. However, an earlier version will not be able to read a later version unless the file has been saved in its format (e.g. Excel 4.0). You can save a spreadsheet file in formats such as:

(a) Template (to create a new template)

(b) Text (.txt)

(c) Microsoft Excel 3.0 (earlier version of Excel)

(d) DBF 4.0 (dbase IV)

8 Save your First Sheet file on to the floppy disk using these formats. Since you have already saved the file once, you need to use the File menu Save As option. The Save As window will appear and if you click on the black triangle button next to Save as type box then a drop-down list of alternative formats will appear (Figure 5.7). You select the new format by double clicking on it. A black triangle button always indicates that a menu or list of other options is available.

9 Change the file name by adding a number (e.g. First Sheet 2 etc.). You may be presented with messages telling you that you may lose data by saving in this format but ignore them. In practice however by making a file readable for other applications you may change its presentation.

10 In order to save the sheet in a format suitable for posting to a website, you need to use the option Save as HTML on the File menu.

11 You can change the appearance of the display using the zoom tool which is provided on the Standard toolbar and as the last item on the View menu. This is exactly the same in all Microsoft

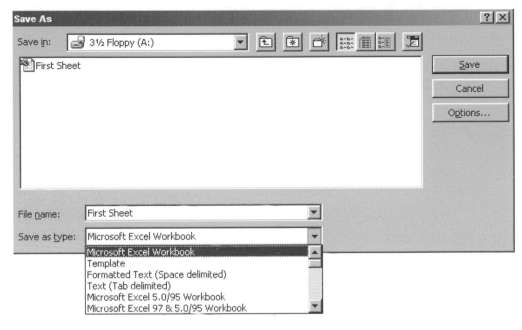

Figure 5.7 Save As window

Office applications (e.g. Word). Figure 4.8 in Chapter 4 shows zoom on the toolbar. You can change the display by clicking on any of the list of options. Within the View menu you will find three other options for changing the display Full Screen, Page Break Review and Normal. Normal is probably the one you are currently using. Explore the options and see which you prefer.

12 You can now close your document by clicking on File and a drop-down menu will reveal an option called Close. Click on Close and the working area will be cleared. If you have made a change to your document since you last saved it then you will be prompted to save the amended document.

TUTORIAL 5.2   Using formulas

First Sheet is essentially a simple chart of financial information and does not illustrate the power of a spreadsheet to manipulate numerical data. In order to turn a spreadsheet into an application to work with numbers rather than presenting them requires the use of formulas. These are mathematical formulas that tell the application how to undertake a calculation. Excel has rules for the construction of formulas. The normal arithmetic symbols change in a spreadsheet so that:

- \+ is addition
- \- is subtraction
- / is division
- * is multiplication

Some examples of formulas are:

A2*5   means that the contents of cell A2 are multiplied by 5

D3*B1	means that the contents of cell D3 are multiplied by the contents of cell B1
C3*A2*10	means that the contents of cell C3 are multiplied by contents of cell A2 and then by 10
F5/3	means that the contents of cell F5 are divided by 3
E7/F6	means that the contents of cell E7 are divided by the contents of cell F6
J11+D6	means that the contents of cell J11 are added to the contents of cell D6
E3-Z12	means that the contents of cell E3 are subtracted from the contents of Z12
H5*4/A1+G6-M22	means that the contents of cell H5 are multiplied by 4; this is then divided by the contents of cell A1, and the contents of cell G6 from which the contents of cell M22 have been subtracted are then added

When your formula consists of several arithmetic operators (e.g. add, multiply, divide or subtract) then Excel works them out according to a standard rule. The application will work out multiplication and division first and addition and subtraction second. If the formula contains both multiplication and division it works out the calculation from left to right.

When you enter your formula, you must start with an equals sign and then enter the formula (e.g. =+D3+D4+D5). This will automatically calculate the formula. If you forget to start with an equals sign, you need to click on the equals sign in the formula bar. A window will

appear to explain the calculation and when you click on the OK button to close the window, you will see the value appear on the spreadsheet.

Excel provides standard functions for regularly used formulas such as totalling a column or a row of figures. This is called SUM. A second frequently used function is AVERAGE which calculates the mean of a range of numbers. You can use both functions by entering formulas such as:

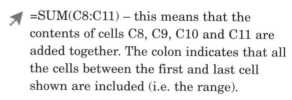

- =SUM(C8:C11) – this means that the contents of cells C8, C9, C10 and C11 are added together. The colon indicates that all the cells between the first and last cell shown are included (i.e. the range).

- =AVERAGE(C8:C11) – this calculates the average of the contents of C8, C9, C10 and C11.

Excel provides an icon for SUM (Figure 5.8) on the Standard toolbar which, if you click on it, will automatically insert the sum formula into your chosen cell.

Figure 5.8 Sum icon

There are a number of error messages that are generated by mistakes in functions and formulas. These are:

######	this occurs when the formula or function produces a number greater than can fit in a cell
#VALUE	the formula contains a mistake in one of its components (i.e. an operand or argument)
#DIV0!	the formula involves being divided by zero
#NAME?	a meaningless term is included in the formula

#N/A	this results from a formula requiring data from a cell which does not contain the information at that moment	#NUM!	an incorrect number in the formula
		#NULL!	formula has an incorrect cell reference
#REF!	the formula has an incorrect cell reference		

Formulas

Duration 60 minutes

1 Load Microsoft Excel and open First Sheet by clicking on File and then Open. The Open window will appear (Figure 5.9). If the floppy drive does not appear in the Look in: box, then click on the down triangle and select the floppy disk from the drop-down list by clicking on it. The First Sheet file will be visible in the working area. This does assume you have inserted your floppy disk in the drive. You can open the file by either single clicking on it and then on the Open button or by double clicking on the file.

2 Enter a formula to provide a total of the three columns C, D and E. In cell C13 enter the formula =C8+C9+C10+C11, click on the cell and enter the text. When you have finished just click elsewhere and you will see the formula

disappear and be replaced by the mathematical answer (i.e. 955). You will notice the formula is shown on the formula bar when you click on the cell (see Figure 5.10). Repeat the process for cell D13 by clicking on the cell and entering =D8+D9+D10+D11.

3 There is an alternative method for adding up a column or row of figures which uses the sum function. You can either enter =SUM(E8:E11) or click on the SUM icon on the Standard toolbar with the column E8 to E13 highlighted. You highlight the group of cells by clicking in E8, holding down the left mouse button and dragging the mouse down the column to E13 then release the button. Using either method provides a total for the column of numbers.

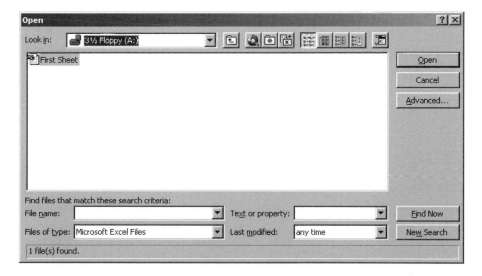

Figure 5.9 Open window

4 Enter totals for each row (i.e. 8, 9,10,11 and 13) by highlighting the row and clicking on the SUM icon. Figure 5.11 shows you the result. It is often difficult to learn how to highlight a group of cells, so continue to practise until you are confident you can carry out the task.

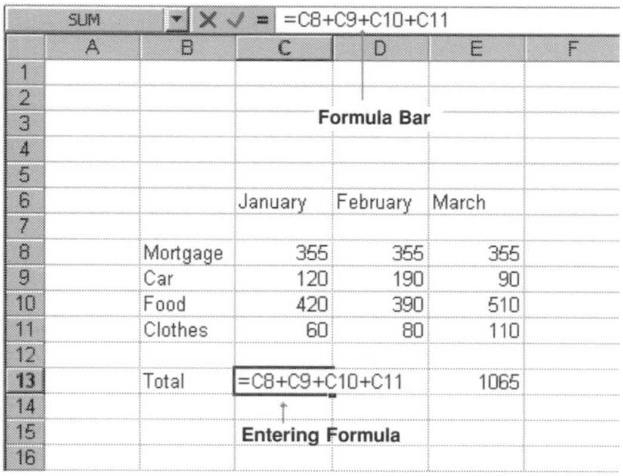

Figure 5.10 Entering formula

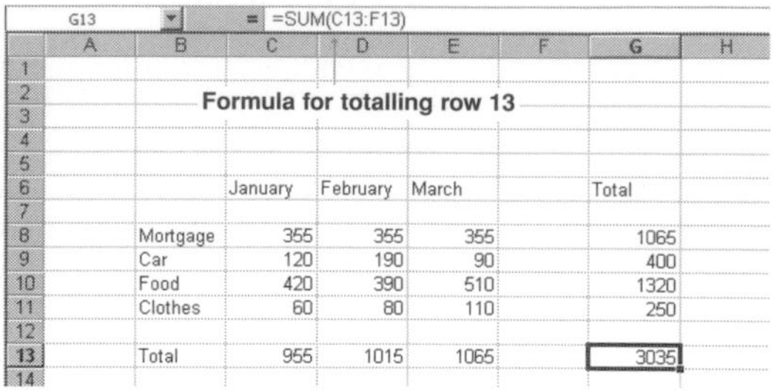

Figure 5.11 Row totals

5 Save the new worksheet on your floppy disk as a file called Second Sheet.

6 Close Excel.

TUTORIAL 5.3   Manipulating a worksheet – 1

Microsoft Excel provides many functions to manipulate your worksheet. Some of them allow you to:

- insert or delete columns;
- insert or delete rows;
- change the width and height of rows and columns;
- change the font of all or part of your worksheet;
- change the size of the font for all or part of your worksheet;
- change the text font colour;
- change the text by emboldening, italics and underlining.

Excel provides you with a range of powerful presentation tools, among the most useful of which are the functions that allow you to insert and remove rows and columns. These are provided in the Insert menu (Figure 5.12). If you click on either of the options (i.e. Rows and Columns) then a new row or column is inserted. In both, the position of the new row or column is dependent on which cell you have highlighted. You can highlight a column or row by clicking on the heading (i.e. letter or number which identifies the row or column). This is useful in helping you pinpoint where you are inserting the new row or column. The new row is placed above the chosen row and the new column is inserted to the left of the chosen column. If you make a mistake then the Undo option can return you to the starting point. To remove a row or column it must be highlighted and the delete option in the Edit menu used.

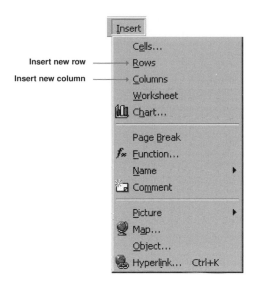

Figure 5.12 Insert rows and columns

The width and depth of rows and columns is not fixed and can be changed. Figure 5.13 illustrates that you can either manually or automatically adjust the width and height of a column and row using the options within the Format menu.

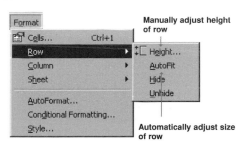

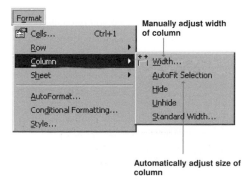

Figure 5.13 Adjust width and depth

You can also drag the width of columns and height of rows using the mouse pointer. Figure 5.14 shows that if you place the mouse pointer over a gap between rows or columns they will change shape. If the left mouse button is held down, you are able to drag the column edge to make it wider or to make the row deeper.

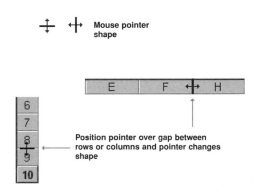

Figure 5.14 Drag rows and columns

The Formatting toolbar is similar to that provided in Word in that you can change fonts and the size of the characters. Figure 5.15 illustrates where options are provided as a list beneath the toolbar. You select the new font or size by clicking on it. Further along the toolbar (Figure 5.16) you have access to options that will embolden, underline, change text into italics and provide colour highlights and fonts.

The formatting toolbar (Figure 5.16) also has five functions called styles that allow you to change the number styles in a cell. Right to left these styles are as follows:

- Currency – inserts a pounds sign and presents the numbers as pounds and pence.

- Percent – inserts a percentage sign.

- Comma – the number is displayed using commas.

- Increase – increases the number behind the decimal point.

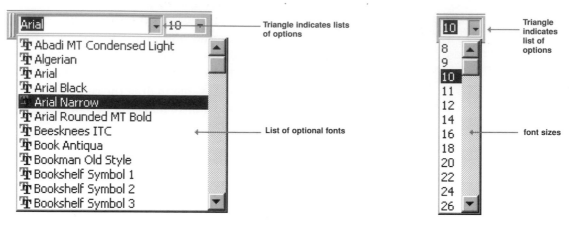

Figure 5.15 Fonts and character sizes

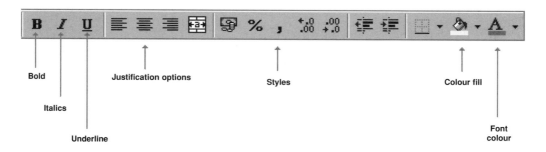

Figure 5.16 Formatting toolbar

 Decrease – decreases the number behind the decimal point.

These styles are used by highlighting the cells you want to change and then clicking on the toolbar function.

Change your worksheet's presentation

Duration 60 minutes

Exercise 5.3

1 Load Excel and open Second Sheet file from your floppy disk.

2 Delete rows 1 to 4 by clicking in cell A1 and holding down the left mouse button. Drag the pointer into A4 and release the button. Cells A1, A2, A3 and A4 are now highlighted. Click on Edit to create a drop-down menu. Click on option Delete and a small window will appear (Figure 5.17). Since we are removing entire rows, click on the radio button next to Entire row and then click the OK button. If you highlight entire rows rather than individual cells then the Delete window will not appear since you have already selected entire rows.

3 Insert a new row between mortgage, car, food and clothes rows by highlighting a cell in the car row. Click on Insert menu and a drop-down menu appears with the option Rows. Click on Rows and you will see a new row appear between the mortgage and car rows. Repeat this process to produce the layout in Figure 5.18.

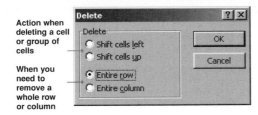

Action when deleting a cell or group of cells

When you need to remove a whole row or column

Figure 5.17 Delete window

	A	B	C	D	E	G	H
1							
2			January	February	March		Total
3							
4		Mortgage	355	355	355		1065
5							
6		Car	120	190	90		400
7							
8		Food	420	390	510		1320
9							
10		Clothes	60	80	110		250
11							
12		Total	955	1015	1065		3035
13							

Figure 5.18 Insert rows

4 Insert a new column between column B and C. Click on the column C heading to highlight the entire column. Click on Insert menu and then the Column option. A new column will be inserted between the two.

5 Highlight row 2 (i.e. the one containing the headings January, February, March and Total) and, using the font and size options on Formatting toolbar, change the headings to Ariel size 16 font. Highlight column B (i.e. containing mortgage, car, food and clothes) and, using font and size options on the Formatting toolbar (Figure 5.15), change the titles to Ariel size 12.

6 Highlight row 2 and column B and embolden the text using the Formatting toolbar (Figure 5.16) options. Figure 5.19 shows the outcomes of these changes. You will notice that the column width is too narrow to show January and February and that words such as 'Mortgage' overlap into the next cell. To adjust the size of the columns highlight the whole area by clicking in cell B2

and, holding mouse button down, move the pointer to I13, then release the button. Click on Format and then position pointer on Column option to reveal the sub-menu, then click on AutoFit Selection. The layout will now change (Figure 5.20).

	A	B	C	D	E	F	H	I
1								
2				Janua	Febru	March		Total
3								
4		Mortgage		355	355	355		1065
5								
6		Car		120	190	90		400
7								
8		Food		420	390	510		1320
9								
10		Clothes		60	80	110		250
11								
12		Total		955	1015	1065		3035
13								

Figure 5.19 New layout

B	C	D	E	F	H	I
		January	February	March		Total
Mortgage			355	355	355	1065
Car			120	190	90	400
Food			420	390	510	1320
Clothes			60	80	110	250
Total			955	1015	1065	3035

Figure 5.20 Autofit revised

7 The final step to improve the presentation of the worksheet is to change the colour of the column titles. Highlight the row 2 and click on the triangle directly to the right of the font colour icon on the Formatting toolbar. A palette of colours will appear for you to select. Choose one and you will see the column titles change to the selected colour.

8 Save the spreadsheet as Third Sheet on your floppy disk.

9 Close Excel.

► TUTORIAL 5.4 Manipulating a worksheet – 2

Microsoft Excel has several functions that allow you to manipulate your worksheet. Some of them let you:

- cut or copy the contents of cells to new areas of your worksheet;
- automatically fill cells or increment data;
- sort numerical data;
- align cell contents;
- add a border to parts of your worksheet;
- search and replace cell contents.

Excel contains options (that are also available in Word) of copying and cutting areas of the sheet and moving them to new areas. It is also possible to copy material from other Microsoft Office applications into a worksheet. The options are provided on the Standard toolbar and in the Edit menu in the same positions as in Word. Figure 4.15 in Chapter 4 illustrates these options. In order to use the Copy, Cut and Paste options you need to highlight the area of the sheet you intend to work on and then select either Copy or Cut. Copy leaves the selected area unchanged while Cut removes the contents.

You may have noticed that when you highlight a cell, the bottom right-hand corner takes the form of a square. When the mouse pointer is positioned over the square which is called the fill handle, the pointer changes to a black cross. If you hold down the left mouse button and drag the handle, you can copy the contents of the cell to the adjacent cells. If the contents of the original cell are part of a natural sequence (e.g. Monday, Tuesday, Wednesday etc.) then the new cell will be filled by the next step in the sequence. This works with numbers, dates or times and is called autofilling. Figure 5.21 illustrates using Autofill to copy a sequence of the days of the week.

The justification of the cell contents can be adjusted using the functions provided on the Formatting toolbar. These are the same as those provided in Word and they are illustrated in Figure 4.22 in Chapter 4. They allow you to left, right, centre or full justify the contents of a cell. Excel provides an alternative way of justifying the contents which also gives

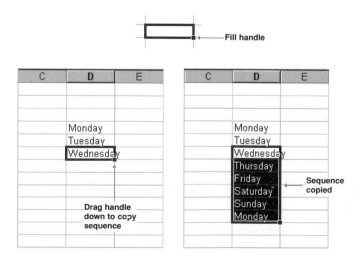

Figure 5.21 Autofill

you access to other formatting functions. In the Format menu there is an option Cells which, if you click on it, opens the Format Cells window (Figure 5.22). This is a tabbed window in that if you click on the various tabs, you are given access to other functions.

For example

- Tab – Alignment allows you to justify the contents and orientation of a cell both horizontally and vertically.

- Tab – Font provides you with an alternative way to choose of fonts, sizes and styles to that which the Formatting toolbar offers.

- Tab – Borders allows you to enclose cells with a border of your choice.

Excel also provides you with two functions to sort information. You can sort numerical data into ascending or descending order or text into alphabetical order. These functions are available on the Standard toolbar (Figure 5.23) as two icons (an arrow pointing up or down). They operate in the same way as other functions in that the selected information is highlighted and then the chosen icon is selected.

Another useful presentation feature of a spreadsheet is that you can enclose the cells within a border. The process is similar to other functions in that the first step is to highlight the area of the sheet to which you want to add a border and then you select a border by clicking on the border icon (Figure 5.23). This opens a small window with a number of options. By clicking on an option you will see it applied to your highlighted area.

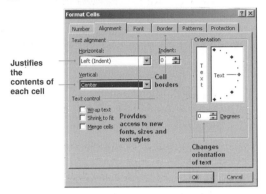

Figure 5.22 Format Cells window

An important function is to be able to search a spreadsheet to locate distinct information and to replace it if necessary. This is an identical function to that available in Word. The function is an option within the Edit menu and available as a straightforward Find or a Find and Replace option. Figure 5.24 illustrates the Find and Replace window which is opened when you click on the option in the menu. This provides you with a range of choices, including replace each individual item or replace them all.

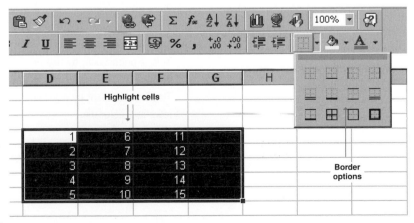

Figure 5.23 Borders

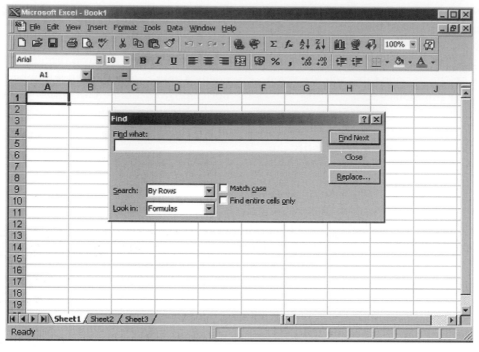

Figure 5.24 Find and Replace

Change the worksheet

Duration 30 minutes

Exercise 5.4

1 Load Excel and open Third Sheet file from your floppy disk.

2 Re-order the layout so that the cost items are arranged in alphabetical order (i.e. Car, Clothes, Food and Mortgage), using the cut and paste functions. This is achieved by highlighting the row and using the functions on the Standard toolbar (Figure 5.25). Cut the highlighted row and paste it into its new position.

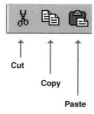

Cut

Copy

Paste

Figure 5.25 Cut and Paste

3 Use the Autofill function to extend the top row of the sheet to include April, May and June. Highlight the row (i.e. January, February and March) and use the handle to drag the highlight to extend the months. This will obscure the Total Heading and make the total column meaningless, so insert a new Total (i.e. L2) and move the column to place it under the heading.

4 Use the Borders icon to enclose the spreadsheet. This is undertaken by highlighting the whole area, clicking on Borders icon and selecting a border. Tidy up the sheet by removing any unnecessary rows and columns.

5 Fill the new columns you have created with the following information and total the columns using the Sum function:

	April	May	June
Car	100	120	80
Clothes	80	60	54
Food	345	289	564
Mortgage	355	355	355

6 Figure 5.26 illustrates the final view of the sheet although this depends on which rows or columns you choose to remove.

7 Save the spreadsheet as Fourth Sheet on your floppy disk.

8 Close Excel.

	January	February	March	April	May	June	Total
Car	120	190	90	100	120	80	500
Clothes	60	80	110	80	60	54	330
Food	420	390	510	345	289	564	1665
Mortgage	355	355	355	355	355	355	1420
Total	955	1015	1065	880	824	1053	3915

Figure 5.26 Final View of Sheet

TUTORIAL 5.5   Printing

Many spreadsheets will be used as printed documents and the impact of a printed sheet relies on its presentation. Excel provides an overall means of setting up the page layout in order to establish margins and page orientation (i.e. portrait or landscape), add headers and footers to the sheet and decide what parts of the spreadsheet should be printed. This is available in the File menu (Figure 5.27) within the Page Setup option (Figure 5.28).

The Page Setup window offers four tabbed pages. These are as follows.

* Page – this allows you to select the orientation of the page (i.e. landscape or portrait).

* Margins – this lets you to set the margins (i.e. top, bottom, right and left).

* Header/Footer – you can create a header and footer for the sheet.

* Sheet – this allows you to determine what parts of the sheet are printed and in what order.

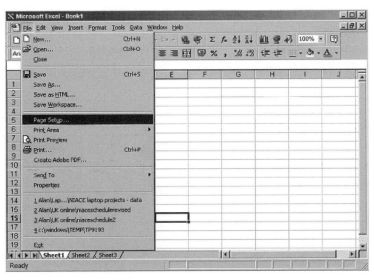

Figure 5.27 File menu

The File menu also provides you with other useful options including:

- Print Area – this enables you to set areas of the sheet you want to print by initially highlighting them and then using this option to identify them for printing.

- Print Preview – this shows how your selections will look once printed. It is very useful in checking the layout of your printed document before you waste any paper.

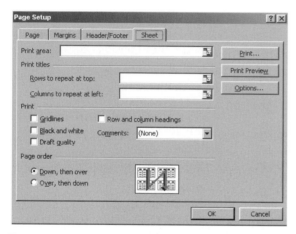

Figure 5.28 Page Setup

Once you are content with the layout of the document you can print it by using the File menu option Print or by clicking on the print icon (Figure 5.29) on the Standard toolbar. This is the same process as print a Word document or any other product of a Microsoft Office application. Once you click on Print then you access the Print Controller as illustrated in Figure 5.30.

Figure 5.29 Print icon

The print controller allows you to select:

- how many copies of the document you want to print;

- which pages of the document to print (you can print any combination of pages);

- which parts of a sheet to print;

- what printer to use (this assumes you have more than one connected);

- whether to collate the printed pages or not.

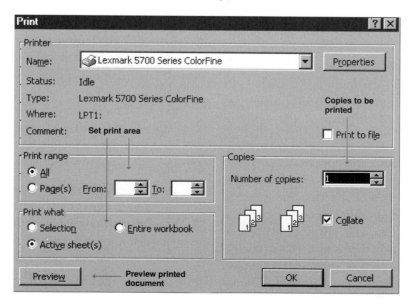

Figure 5.30 Print Controller

TUTORIAL 5.6   Charts and graphs

The spreadsheet is essentially a way of modelling or presenting numerical information in an understandable form. Many spreadsheets including Excel provide you with the means of turning your sheets into more visual representations such as pie charts, bar charts and histograms. In order to turn a sheet or a part of a sheet into a chart requires the area to be highlighted and then the Chart Wizard to be activated. The Chart Wizard is launched by clicking on the icon (Figure 5.31) on the Standard toolbar.

Using the Wizard (Figure 5.32) you can select from a large number of alternative charts and graphs. By simply choosing a chart or graph and following the wizard's instructions the data is converted into this new representation. The Wizard allows you to preview the different charts and graphs.

You can also insert images and files from other Microsoft Office applications into your spreadsheets using the options available within the Insert menu. These are shown in Figure 5.12, and the main options being Picture and Object. This is undertaken in an identical manner to importing pictures or files into Word. If you study Tutorial 4.2 and Exercise 4.2 in Chapter 4 you will see how to use the functions within Excel.

Figure 5.31 Excel Chart Wizard icon

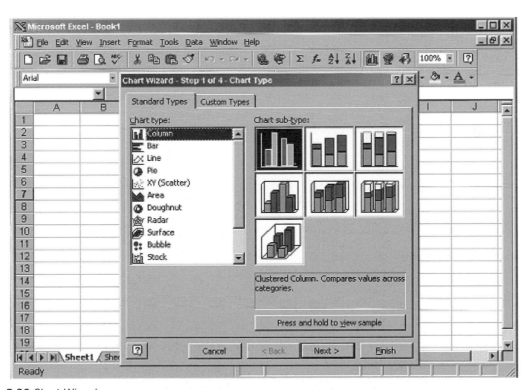

Figure 5.32 Chart Wizard

Exercise 5.5

Creating charts and graphs

Duration 45 minutes

1 Load Excel and open Fourth Sheet file from your floppy disk.

2 Highlight the area of the numerical table of information and click on the Chart Wizard Icon and you will see the wizard open.

3 Explore the different charts by single clicking on each option in turn, both Standard and Custom types and then click on the 'Press and hold to view sample' button holding the mouse button down to preview the chart. This way you can see each chart's representation of the sheets data.

4 When you have explored the different options select one that you feel is a good presentation and create it by following the wizard instructions.

5 The chart or graph you have selected will appear on your sheet surrounded by a rectangle which allows you to change the shape of the chart by dragging the edges using the mouse. Practise moving the chart around and changing its size.

You can remove the surrounding rectangle by clicking away from the chart and reimpose the rectangle by single clicking on the chart. If you need to delete the chart you first need to re-establish the rectangle and then press the delete key. Within the chart you can highlight individual objects and similarly modify and change them.

6 Within the View menu the toolbar options provide access to a special Chart toolbar. This provides you with several functions to change your chart in many ways. You click on the chart to highlight it and then the functions can be applied. They allow you to change the type of chart, fonts, colours, legends and position of objects. Explore these functions until you are confident.

7 Save the spreadsheet with the chart as Fifth Sheet on your floppy disk.

8 Close Excel.

Databases

By the end of this chapter you should be able to:

- open and close a database application;

- save a database;

- use Help function;

- modify database application settings;

- design and plan a database;

- create a database including a table;

- enter, modify and delete data and records in a table;

- create and modify a form for data entry;

- create and use different types of queries;

- create, modify and use a report.

The chapter covers Module 4 of the ECDL syllabus. It is divided into tutorials which include exercises that will allow you to practise many of the concepts presented in the text. Each exercise indicates how long it should take you to complete. They can be undertaken anywhere you can gain access to a computer – work, college, a local library, learning centre or at home.

The tutorials in this chapter are as follows:

TUTORIAL 6.1 What is a database?

A database is a way of organising information so that it is easy to search it to find particular items or groups of items. The modern world is full of databases although in many cases this is not obvious. When you telephone your bank, they search their database to locate the records of your account so that they can answer your queries. Almost everyone who sends you a bill (e.g. gas, electricity, council tax and credit cards) holds the information on a database so that in many ways society is a collection of databases. This has both advantages and disadvantages. It makes it straightforward to make banking transactions over the telephone, to buy goods by credit card and many other things. However, it also means that people can

find out where you live, check on your credit worthiness and discover information you may regard as personal.

The Data Protection Act is intended to prevent people exploiting the power of the computer to hold information about you without an acceptable reason. Data users are required to register what they are doing and their reasons for doing it. It is a criminal offence if they fail to register or they work outside their registration. The initial act was passed in 1984 but has been replaced by the 1998 Act (http://www.hmso.gov.uk provides access to the Act) which seeks to harmonise the law across Europe.

A database contains tables of individual records which are themselves divided into fields. Figure 6.1 shows a table, records and fields. In this example the staff number is a unique identifier of each row or record of the table which is known as the Primary Key. This is an important attribute in that it offers a way of relating this table with others so that the information they contain can be related to each other.

A table is called a database object. There are other database objects called queries, forms, reports, macros and modules. Queries provide you with facilities to ask questions and to sort the information held in the database. Forms assist you to edit, enter and view the database information. Reports are a means of extracting information in a preferred format so you can print and distribute it to other users. Macros are a way of automating certain standard functions. It can perform any task you normally would undertake using a keyboard and mouse (e.g. print a particular report). A module holds visual basic code which allows you to customise your database.

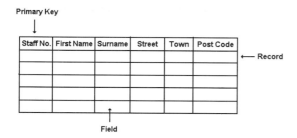

Figure 6.1 Table

You will encounter databases in many different situations and in most cases you will be able to use them to find information or to relate one piece of information to another. However, you will probably be unable to change their structure or even add new data to them. This is because the designer of the database has constructed a read-only version. This is rather like a book – you can read the book and use its contents but you cannot add new material to it. In other cases, the designer will restricted your ability to change the structure of the database but allow you to add new information to the system and use the contents. This is typical of databases which you will encounter at work. This flexibility is provided to allow databases to meet the needs of their users. There are a range of database applications which are provided to build these different types of databases.

Microsoft Access is a modern system designed to construct relational databases. A relational database is one in which each group of records (a table) relates to other tables of information. In contrast to a relational database is a flat file database which is rather like a card index in that it contains tables of information which are separated from each other. This is still a useful form of database but is limited and does not allow you to construct complex structures of information. Relational databases are useful in that you are able to link different tables of information together so many modern databases are relational. Tables can relate to each other in two main ways:

- one item in the initial table relates to many items in the next table;
- many items in the initial table relate to many items in the next table.

If you consider a family of a father, mother and three children (one boy and two girls) then relationships are complex and are similar to the relationships between tables. In the family there are many relationships including:

- mother to father   one-to-one
- mother to children   one-to-many
- brother to sisters   one-to-many

⬈ parents to son   many-to-one

⬈ children to parents   many-to-many

Relationships are a key feature of relational databases since they allow you to search for particular combinations of information. During the design of a database you need to establish relationships.

▶ TUTORIAL 6.2   The basics

When you first click on the Microsoft Access icon on the Windows Desktop or launch it from the Programs menu, the first display you see is shown in Figure 6.2.

This reveals three main choices:

⬈ Create a new database (Blank Database)

⬈ Create a new database using the Wizard help system

⬈ Open an existing database

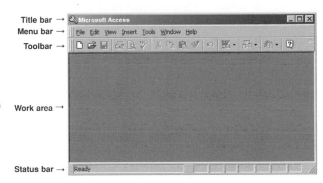

Figure 6.3 Microsoft Access window

A key feature of the application are the toolbars which provide the functions to create and manipulate your database. You have access to a number of different toolbars providing many different functions. Figure 6.4 shows the database and web toolbars. Compare these with those provided by Word and Excel. Although there are many similarities, there are some important differences. In order to use these different functions, you have to change the toolbars.

Figure 6.2 Opening display in Microsoft Access

These options are offered in a window over the work area of the Microsoft Access Window which is shown in Figure 6.3. This looks very like the other Microsoft Office applications you have previously studied. It shows the different bars and the familiar work area of Microsoft Office applications.

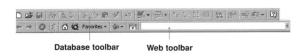

Database toolbar   Web toolbar

Figure 6.4 Database and Web toolbars

To do this you need to click on the View menu (Figure 6.5) option which reveals a drop-down menu containing the option Toolbar. If you click on Toolbar then a list of possible toolbars are provided. Those which have been selected are indicated by having a tick alongside their names. A toolbar can be removed by clicking on the option and the tick and toolbar will be removed. To add a new toolbar simply click on the one you need. A tick appears alongside and it is made available. This method of changing toolbars is identical to all Microsoft Office applications (see Chapter 4). The new toolbar is either inserted into the others at the top of the application or displayed as a box. You can add the free toolbox to the bars by dragging and releasing it over the existing ones. Access provides two standard toolbars (i.e. Database and Web) and a facility to produce a customised one.

All Microsoft Office applications provide an identical Help function. It is accessed and used in the same way in all applications and was explained in Tutorial 4.2 in Chapter 4. The Help function is located on the menu bar of Access. If you click on the Help menu item then Figure 6.6 will appear. If you click on the Contents and Index option you will be presented with a list of the contents of the Help function. You search the list by entering a word in the top box.

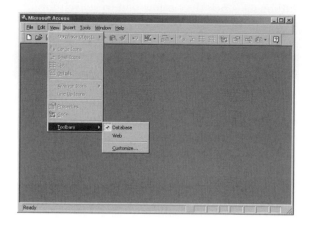

Figure 6.5 Access View menu

Figure 6.6 Microsoft Access Help menu

Open Microsoft Access

Duration 15 minutes

Exercise 6.1

1 Load Microsoft Access by double clicking on the Access icon (Figure 6.7) on the desktop or by clicking on Start, selecting Programs and then clicking on Microsoft Access. Figure 6.3 shows the database application in a window. If your computer displays the application in a window, expand it to fill the screen by using the maximise button in top right-hand corner of the window

Figure 6.7 Microsoft Access icon

2 When the application opens (Figure 6.2) you will be presented with two choices. These are to create a new database (i.e. a blank database or using a Wizard) or open an existing database. For the moment, click on the cancel button to close this window, leaving an empty Microsoft Access window (Figure 6.3).

3 Explore the various menu and toolbar icons. Many of these items are greyed out indicating that they are not available but systematically click on each menu item and look at what is revealed.

Figure 6.8 shows the file menu. You should familarise yourself with the options under each menu.

Figure 6.8 File menu

4 You can now close Access by clicking on File and a drop-down menu will reveal an option called Exit. Click on Exit and the application will close. The alternative is to close the application window using the standard buttons in the top right-hand corner of the window.

TUTORIAL 6.3   Creating a new database

You will be helped to create a straightforward database for keeping staff records. This will contain three tables of records holding personal, salary and training information. The temptation is to launch Microsoft Access immediately and start building the database, but it is far better to plan your database before trying to develop it. This will save you a lot of time and will ensure your final product is suitable.

include and what the system must be able to do. If we assume we have done this analysis, then the items (i.e. fields) are:

- staff numbers, title, first name, surname, street, town and postcode

- job title and salary

- induction, basic computing, word-processing, spreadsheets, databases, management 1 and management 2

First step

The first step is to decide what information your database will hold. Individual items of information are called fields. If we consider personal, salary and training records then what fields will we need? In practice you will need to consult your colleagues who will be using the system to find out what they want to

Second step

Next you need to identify what type of data each field will hold. The main types are as follows.

- Text – this is probably the commonest type of data and a text field can hold up to 256 characters which can be letters, numbers or special characters. You determine how long the field is.

- Memo – this allows you to store large files of information. You could use it to store customers' comments, special information or descriptions of products.

- Numbers – this allows fields to hold numbers so that the database can perform calculations on these fields (e.g. divide annual salary by 12 to automatically calculate monthly pay).

- Date/time – this provides a standard format for inserting dates and times (i.e. —/—/—).

- Currency – this holds information about money which can be used in calculations. This field has been customised for currency and so works more efficiently than a number field.

- Autonumber – this field allows an unique number to be inserted to be used to number records.

- Yes/No – a simple field holding either a yes or no (e.g. has the person attended the training course – yes or no?).

- OLE object – this provides the means of including in the database other windows objects (e.g. graphic image). When you click on the object, the appropriate application is opened and you can view that object.

- Hyperlink – this enables you to link the database to a website.

If we consider the fields we intend to create then we can decide what data types each will be. Table 6.1 relates the fields with an appropriate data type.

Field name	Data type
Staffnumber	Autonumber – this field will automatically be incremented for each new member of staff
Title	Text – 4 characters
First name	Text – 15 characters
Surname	Text – 25 characters
Street	Text – 25 characters
Town	Text – 20 characters
Postcode	Text – 8 characters
Jobtitle	Text
Title	Text
Salary	Currency
Induction	Yes/No
Basic Computing	Yes/No
Word-processing	Yes/No
Spreadsheets	Yes/No
Database	Yes/No
Management 1	Yes/No
Management 2	Yes/No

Table 6.1 Data types

In practice, you not only need to consider the data type, but also all the other features of a database system including:

- input forms

- queries

- reports

However, in order to provide an uncluttered tutorial, we will deal with these aspects later in the chapter.

▶ **Creating tables**

Duration 60 minutes

1 Open Microsoft Access and select 'create a new database' using a blank database and click on OK. This leads you to a display in which you can name your new database and create a new folder to store it in. Figure 6.9 shows the window which appears.

Figure 6.9 Open New Database

Although you do not need to open a new folder, it is good practice to store each database in a separate one. If you decide to do so, then click on the new folder button and create a folder called Staff. You will see this appear in the working area of the window. In order to store your blank database you need to open the folder by clicking on its icon then name your file. You do this by entering a name in the File name box. Clicking on the create button completes the process.

2 Once you have clicked on Create, a new window shown in Figure 6.10 appears which allows you to develop the objects that make up the database. To select a particular object, you click on the Tab and then New.

3 Create a new table by selecting the Tables tab and then the New button. A new window will appear (Figure 6.11) which provides you with different views of the table. Select Design View and click on the OK button. The window shown in Figure 6.12 will appear. In the column called Field Name, enter the personal fields shown in

Table 6.1. They are Staffnumber, Title, First name, Surname, Street, Town and Postcode. As you enter each name, click on the next column (Data Type) and a small button with a down arrow will appear. If you click on this button, a list of data types will appear from which you can select. Choose the types from Table 6.1.

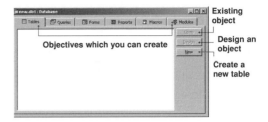

Figure 6.10 Objects window

Once you have entered all the field's names and data types then it is useful to enter a few words to describe the nature of the field. For the Staffnumber entry write 'Unique Primary Key' since this is going to be defined as the table's primary key. To define the field as a primary key you need to click on the primary key icon (Figure 6.12) on the toolbar while the cursor is in the Staffnumber row. As soon as you do this, a key appears in left-hand margin of the row (Figure 6.13).

Figure 6.11 Table views

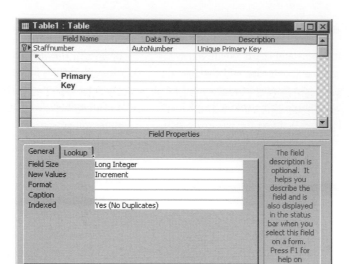

Figure 6.12 Fields and Data Types

Figure 6.13 Primary Key

4 In the bottom half of the Field Data Type window (Figure 6.12) you will see a row called Field Size. For Staffnumber it will show Long Integer. This is because this field has a numeric data type which can take a variety of forms. An integer is a whole number between −32768 and +32767 while a long integer is any whole number. For each field change the field size to the ones shown in Table 6.1. You must have your cursor in the appropriate row.

5 You now need to save your table by clicking on File in the Menu bar and selecting Save. You will need to name your table as part of the process. Try to be consistent in your names as it will help you recall them later. Name this table 'Staffnumber'. You will now return to the Object

creation window (Figure 6.10) which will show a table Staffnumber. If you highlight this icon and click on Open, you will see the results of your efforts. It should resemble Figure 6.14.

This lets you to see what your table looks like and is called the datasheet view. Only one row is shown because you have not entered any data into the table yet. As you enter data, the table will expand.

6 In order to amend or add to this table, you need to close the datasheet and open the table by clicking on design button. You will then return to Figure 6.12 which gives you a view of the Fields and Data Types. You can insert new fields in any place in the table, delete a field, change the order of the fields by moving them and alter which field is the Primary key.

7 To insert a new field in the table, click on the left-hand margin of the row below where you would

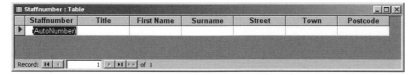

Figure 6.14 Datasheet View of the Staffnumber

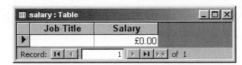

Figure 6.15 Other tables

like to insert the new field and then click on the menu bar item Insert and select Rows. A new blank line will appear and you can enter the new field. If you make a mistake then use the Undo (Edit menu item) facility to remove the entry.

To remove a field, click on the left-hand margin of the designated field so that is highlighted and click on the menu item Edit and select Delete. The row will be removed. You can again use Undo if you make a mistake.

To move a field (i.e. change layout of the table) you must again highlight the field row you want to change. You can now drag the row to the new position.

To select a new primary key field you must first highlight the new row and then click on the Primary Key button on the Toolbar. If you want to remove the the primary key from the table then click on the existing primary key row and then on the icon.

Explore these features until you are confident that you can change fields and layout of a table.

8 You can now create the last two tables of this database. The first step is to determine the fields you intend to create, then you can decide what data types each will be. Figure 6.15 illustrates the two possible tables.

9 The next step is to add data to these tables. This is achieved by opening each table in turn and clicking in the field in which you wish to enter information. The data can then simply be typed into the field. When a record is completed you can move to the next one by pressing enter (return) and a new record (i.e. row) is opened. When you have completed a table then Save the information by clicking on the File menu and selecting the Save option.

10 To change an entry then click on the field and delete it using the keyboard and then re-enter the information.

11 Save your work and close Access. Both save and close functions are available on the File menu.

▶ TUTORIAL 6.4 Using a database

Microsoft Access is provided with a sample database called Northwind Traders (Figure 6.16), an option that can be installed with the main program. If you find your copy of Access has been installed without Northwind, you can add it from your master CD-ROM. Instructions are available in the Help function under the Northwind sample database item.

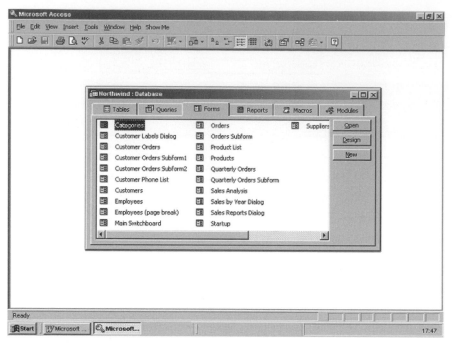

Figure 6.16 Northwind Traders sample database

Figure 6.17 is the Northwind database window. This illustrates the different tables which make up the database. If you click on the other tabs (e.g. queries, forms, reports, macros and modules) you will discover the other elements of the database. It is important to explore the different elements as each serves a key role. These are:

- queries – this is the method of interrogating the information contained in the database and it is also the means of changing the presentation of the information;

- forms – this is a way of entering data into a database; it involves designing a form to help users know what information is required;

- reports – these are used to output information from the database in a useful form; they can be based on the results of a query;

- macros – this is a small program which instructs Access to carry out certain tasks such as produce a report or query the database; it allows you to automate tasks;

- modules – these are Visual Basic programs which allow you to instruct Access to carry out tasks which are not possible through other means.

Figure 6.17 Northwind database window

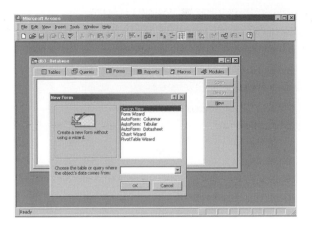

Figure 6.18 New Form

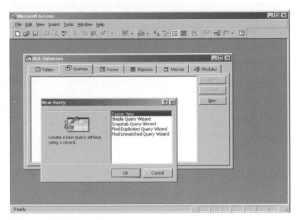

Figure 6.19 New Query

Access allows you to create three types of forms:

◢ columnar

◢ tabular

◢ datasheet

From the Database window (Figure 6.17), click on the Forms tab and then on the New button. The New Form window (Figure 6.18) will open. This shows the three types of form.

Access provides you with many types of query, and each one serves a different purpose:

◢ Select query – allows you to view selected records and fields from a single table.

◢ Crosstab query – lets you change the display of data so that it is easier to compare and contrast the information.

◢ Make-table query – creates a new table with the results of the query.

◢ Append query – lets you append the data in one table on to the information in another table.

◢ Delete query – enables you to delete all the records within a table.

From the Database window (Figure 6.17), click on the Query tab and then on the New button. The New Query Window (Figure 6.19) will open, showing the Query wizards which enable you to create queries. These can be complex.

Another way of sorting through the information contained in a table is to use a filter rather than a query. Filtering allows you to select data which complies with one or more criteria. For example sorting out all the female staff who are aged over 30 and have worked for the company for more than five years. When you are working within the table you can select a field by placing your mouse pointer in the field and then clicking on the Filter by Selection icon on the toolbar (i.e you are selecting each filter criteria one-by-one). Figures 6.20 and 6.21 illustrates the process of filtering by selection. You are sorting or filtering out all the records with the product Mozzarella di Giovanni. The filter can be removed by clicking on the Apply Filter icon on the toolbar. Figure 6.22 also shows the Filter by Form icon that allows you to include a filter in a form.

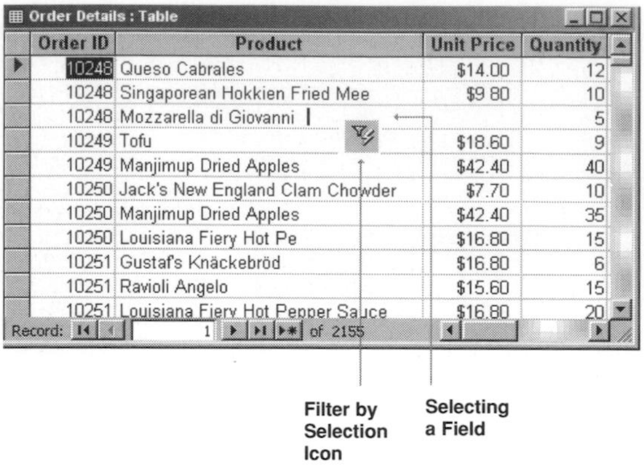

Figure 6.20 Filtering by Selection

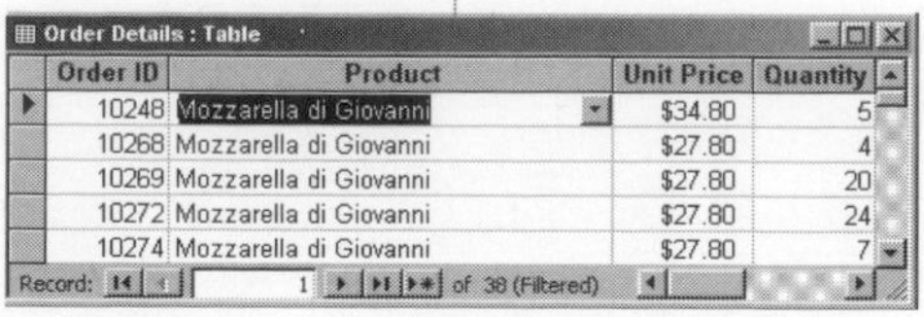

Filter by
Selection
Icon

Selecting
a Field

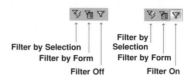

Figure 6.21 Results of the filter showing all records with chosen field

Filter by Selection

Filter by Form

Filter by
Selection

Filter by Form

Filter Off

Filter On

Filter 6.22 Filter On and Off

Exercise 6.3

Using an existing database

Duration 60 minutes

1 Open Microsoft Access and you will be offered a variety of choices as shown in Figure 6.23. You are aiming to open the Northwind Traders database and there is a variety of methods to achieve this result. If, as in Figure 6.23, Northwind is shown in the display you can double click on it to launch the database. If it is absent, you can select Open an existing database or double click on More files. In both cases you will be presented with the Open Window which allows you to locate Northwind by browsing the folder structure. When you locate Northwind it can be loaded by double clicking on the file. Figure 6.24 illustrates the likely location of Northwind on your computer.

2 When Northwind is launched you are initially presented with Figure 6.17 and by clicking on OK the Northwind Database window is opened. Explore the database by working through the various tables to investigate their contents. Try to locate an employee called Dodsworth and find out how old she is; what category of food are Carnarvon Tigers; who is the company contact for customer ID QUEDE and in what city is the supplier Leka Trading based.

3 Explore the Queries, Forms and Records – these provide many examples.

4 Open the Form Employees which provides information on the nine employees of Northwind Traders and add a tenth employee by moving through the Form (Figure 6.25). The details are:

John Gordon, Sales Representative. He reports to Steven Buchanan and was hired on 23 July 2000. His extension is 456. John lives at 123 Northgate Street, London, SE3 2HY and his home telephone number is 020 7678 4563. He was born on 28 January 1960 and was awarded a degree in Modern History from Durham University.

Figure 6.23 Existing database

```
    (C:)
      Program Files
        Microsoft Office
          Office
            Samples
              Northwind
```

Figure 6.24 Location of Northwind

5   Once you have entered the information into the form, then open the Table Employees and you should find a new record for John Gordon (Figure 6.26).

6   Now change this record by opening the form again and altering the Personal information box from a degree in Modern History from Durham University to a Masters Degree in Ancient History from Durham University. The approach is to click in the Information box and delete the existing information using the keyboard and then type in the new information. Check the change with the Employees Table.

7   Close and save both the database and Access using the options within the File menu.

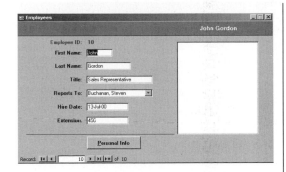

Figure 6.25 New Entry in a form

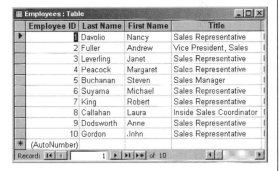

Figure 6.26 New record

Create a new form

Exercise 6.4

Duration 60 minutes

1   Open Microsoft Access and the Northwind Traders database.

2   Once you have cleared the initial Northwind screen display, you will see the Northwind Database window (Figure 6.17). By clicking on the Forms tab you will see the list of existing forms. Explore these by placing your mouse pointer over each one to highlight it and click the Open button. Observe the different styles of forms. They are intended to provide an easy-to-use interface for data entry and editing.

3   The simplest way of producing a form is to use AutoForm. This simply takes the fields in a record and arranges them. In the form view, click on New and Figure 6.18 appears. This shows three different forms of AutoForm, that is, columnar,

tabular and datasheet. In each case you need to select a particular table for which to design a form before the AutoForm function will work. At the bottom of the window (Figure 6.27) there is a drop-down list of tables within the Northwind database. To select a table, you double click on its name in the list. Choose a table and you will see it appear in the box.

4   Once you have chosen a table then use the AutoForm: Columnar option by double clicking on it to create a form. Close this form and create another form using the Autoform: Tabular option and then repeat the process for Autoform: Datasheet. Each form is closed by clicking on the window Close button and declining to save the form when asked by a dialogue box. In this way you can compare the three types of AutoForm.

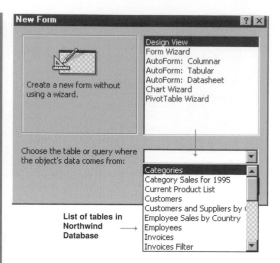

Figure 6.27 Selecting a table for AutoForm

5   Once you have created a form you can amend it by using the design option. From the Form tab display you initially highlight a form and then click on the Design button. The existing form appears in design view (Figure 6.28). This allows you to click in each box to see it enclosed in a box with small rectangles which, when dragged, will change the shape of the box so they can be made larger or smaller. This is a standard windows feature to allow you to move and shape objects.

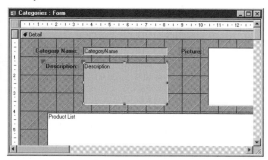

Figure 6.28 Design of forms

6   If you click on a box with text you can change the titles by using the delete keys.

7   With the design window open you can alter the background colour using the AutoFormat option within the Format menu or use the AutoFormat

icon (Figure 6.29) on the toolbar. In both cases the AutoFormat window (Figure 6.30) will appear.

Figure 6.29 AutoFormat icon

8   Access provides a toolbox of options with which you can change forms. These are available in the View menu, Toolbox option (Figure 6.31). This places a toolbox on the screen for you to employ, but it is only available when you are in design view.

9   Using these different options, change the size of a box, alter a text box, change the background and add an image to the form from the Microsoft Clip Gallery.

Figure 6.30 AutoFormat window

10 Close and save both the database and Access using the options within the File menu.

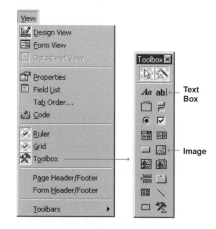

Figure 6.31 Access toolbox

Create a query

Duration 60 minutes

1 Open Microsoft Access and Northwind Traders database.

2 Once you have cleared the initial Northwind screen display the Northwind Database window (Figure 6.17) will appear. By clicking on the Query tab you will see the display of existing queries. Explore these placing your mouse pointer over each one to highlight it and then click the Open button. Observe the different styles of queries. The queries are intended to provide an easy way to find and display the information.

3 Select the Crosstab Query Wizard by double clicking on the item in the list (Figure 6.19) to open the Wizard (Figure 6.32). You need to select the table you are querying by highlighting it and clicking on the Next button. This reveals a window for you to choose the fields you want to make row headings.

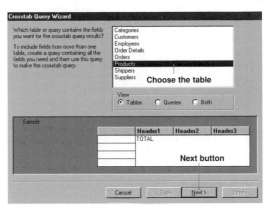

Figure 6.32 Choose the table

4 Figure 6.33 shows the selection of Row headings window. This is achieved by highlighting your choices and clicking on arrow keys. It is possible to reverse the process by highlighting and clicking the arrow in the opposite direction. When you are

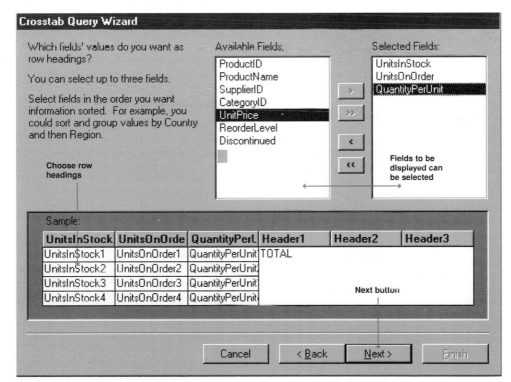

Figure 6.33 Selecting the row headings

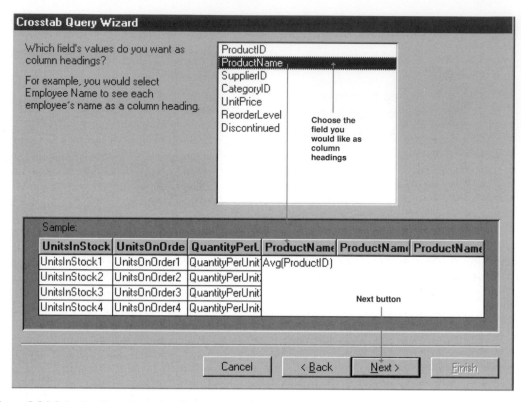

Figure 6.34 Selecting the column headings

finished you must click on Next to open the next window which allows you to select the column heading.

5 Figure 6.34 shows the window for choosing the column headings which are chosen by either double clicking on them or highlighting the field and clicking on the Next button. Another window opens that offers you the choice of a number of different mathematical options which will be applied to the matrix you have created. You select the mathematical option by highlighting it and clicking the Next button. The window closes and the last window in the sequence is opened to allow you to name the query. You can either accept the system's choice of name or insert your own. It also lets you view the results of your query or modify the design.

6 Figure 6.35 illustrates the outcomes of a query.

7 On each window of this wizard sequence you will have noticed a Back button. This provides you with the means of changing your decisions by returning to the previous window and making new decisions.

8 Explore this sequence to create queries by developing different ones.

9 Close both the database and Access using the options within the File menu.

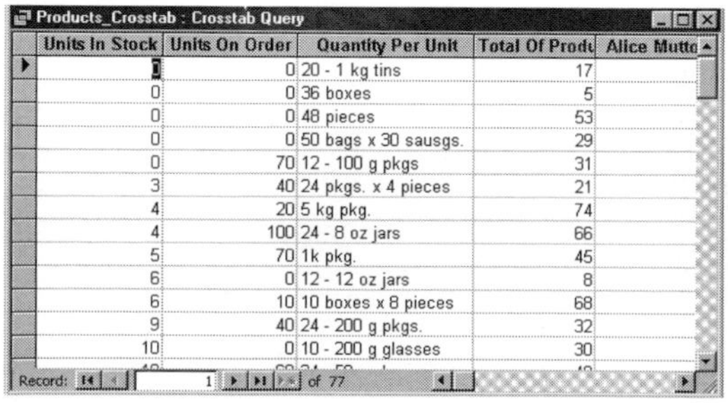

Figure 6.35 Query

TUTORIAL 6.5 Reports

Reports are a way of presenting the outcomes of a database. Forms can also serve this purpose but reports are particularly useful if you need to print the outcome for wider distribution. Access provides a number of different approaches to creating reports (Figure 6.36). These include:

 AutoReports (Columnar and Tabular) – these provide a simple way of accessing content;

 Wizards (Report, Chart and Label) – these are ways whereby the system helps you design reports for different purposes.

AutoReports essentially allow you to choose between two different ways of laying out the report (i.e in columns or tables). The Report Wizard gives you more control over the layout while the label Wizard is essentially used to produce labels for letters and parcels. The Chart Wizard allows you to turn data in your

database into a chart thus providing a different way of presenting the information.

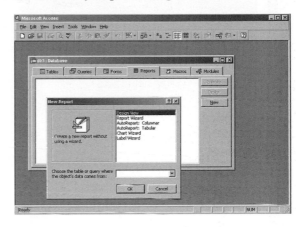

Figure 6.36 New reports

Reports can serve many different purposes. You can create an invoice, a standard sales report for management, stock control documents and many other items, illustrating the value of the database.

Produce a report
Duration 60 minutes

Exercise 6.6

1 Open Microsoft Access and Northwind Traders database.

2 Once you have cleared the initial Northwind screen display you will see the Northwind Database window (Figure 6.17). By clicking on the Report tab you will see the display of existing reports. Explore these by placing your mouse pointer over each one to highlight it and then click the Open button. Observe the different styles of report.

3 In order to create a new report click on New while in the Forms window. The New Report window is opened (Figure 6.36). Select the table about which you wish to create a report and double

click on Report Wizard or highlight it and click on the OK button. The wizard takes you through a sequence of decisions about the nature of the report. These begin with choosing the fields you want to reproduce in the report. You are able to select fields from as many tables as you wish (Figure 6.37).

4 After the fields have been selected then you move on by clicking on Next button. This opens a new window to allow you to group fields together under a common heading so as to display them in this way on the report. Again, you move forward by clicking on the Next button. The next stages (each presented in a separate window) are:

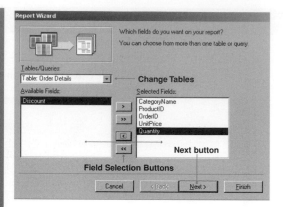

Figure 6.37 Selecting fields for a report

(a) to order the display of the fields;

(b) layout the report from a series of choices (i.e. columnar, tabular, justified, portrait and landscape);

(c) choose from a variety of report styles;

(d) name, preview or modify the report.

Figure 6.38 illustrates a montage of these windows. These are similar to the Query Wizard process.

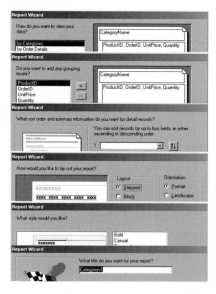

Figure 6.38 Report Wizard montage

5 You have now created a new report. You can see that it has been added to the display of reports in the Report Window. You may find it useful now to modify the layout. You do this by highlighting the report (i.e. the one you have just produced) in the Report Window (similar to Figure 6.17) and then clicking on the Design Button. The new display is shown in Figure 6.39. This is very similar to the Form modify display since the same toolbox is available. The individual display boxes can be changed by clicking inside them so that they are then surrounded by a rectangle which allows you to drag the edges of the box around. The text can be changed and new headers and footers added.

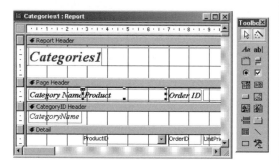

Figure 6.39 Modifying a report

6 Explore the modification process by changing the shape of the form. Position your mouse pointer on the edge of the form (you will see the pointer change shape) and then drag the edge to change its shape. Change the boxes for field information, alter some text and add a new footer (using the Text Box tool in the toolbox).

7 Close both the database and Access using the options within the File menu.

Key features of the application are the toolbars which provide the functions to create, manipulate and format your presentations. So many options are provided that you may need to change them in order to concentrate on different aspects of the process. Figure 7.1 shows the standard and formatting toolbars.

To change a toolbar you have to click on the View menu option which reveals a drop-down menu containing the option Toolbar. If you click on Toolbar then a list of possible toolbars are provided. Figure 7.3 indicates that the standard and formatting toolbar have been selected since a tick is displayed alongside the option. A toolbar can be removed by clicking on the option and the tick and toolbar will be removed. This method of changing the toolbar is identical for all Microsoft Office applications.

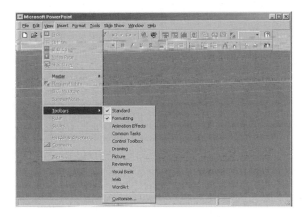

Figure 7.3 Toolbar

All Microsoft Office applications provide an identical Help function. It is accessed and used in the same way. Tutorial 4.2 is provided on the Help function in Chapter 4 so by understanding how to use Help in Microsoft Word you will be able to use the function in PowerPoint. The Help function is located on the menu bar of the applications. If you click on the PowerPoint Help menu item then Figure 7.4 will appear. If you click on the Contents and Index option, you will be

presented with a list of the contents of the Help function. You can search the list by entering a word in the top box.

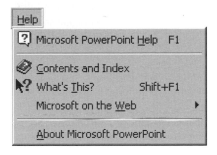

Figure 7.4 PowerPoint Help menu

Another standard function which is common to all Microsoft Office applications is the magnifier or zoom function which lets you increase or decrease the magnification of the work area. This is very useful when you are creating slides in that it allows you to focus on details or view a whole slide which is larger than the display. The magnifier is available on the Standard toolbar and also as an option called Zoom under the View menu. Figure 7.5 illustrates the two routes to the magnifier.

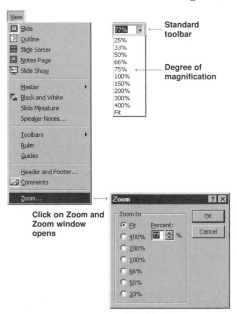

Figure 7.5 Magnification options

▶ **The basics of PowerPoint**   **Duration 90 minutes**

1 Load Microsoft PowerPoint by either double clicking on the PowerPoint icon on the desktop or click on Start and then highlight Programs by placing the mouse pointer on it to reveal menu of options. Click on Microsoft PowerPoint and the application will open to reveal Figure 7.1 with Figure 7.2 on top. This will be either in a window or filling the whole screen.

2 Figure 7.2 asks you to decide whether you want to create a new presentation using:

⤲ AutoContent Wizard

⤲ Template

⤲ Blank presentation

⤲ Open an existing presentation

You need to click on the radio button and then OK to make a selection. Select Blank presentation on this occasion and a small window will open in the working area of the application shown in Figure 7.6.The window consists of many small layouts which are provided for you to choose from. Double click on the option you wish to work on. In this case, select the Title Side shown in Figure 7.6 and the small layout expands in the work area.

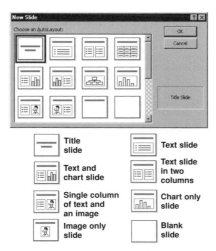

Figure 7.6 New Slide window

3 If you click on one of the boxes you will see that the cursor flashes within it and it is surrounded by an outline with small squares. If you click on them and hold the left mouse button down you can drag the box to change its size and shape. Experiment until you can manipulate the box. Figure 7.7 illustrates these changes.

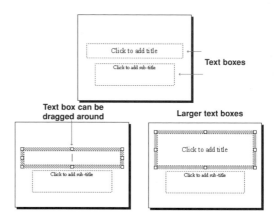

Figure 7.7 Manipulating slides

4 Click in the Add Title box and type, 'Qualifications' then click in the sub-title box and enter 'European Computer Driving Licence'. Your slide should look similar to Figure 7.8.

5 Now explore changing the magnification of the work area, using Zoom in the View menu or the icon on the Standard toolbar.

6 You have created an opening slide for a presentation but you will normally need several slides. To add another you need to click on Insert and New slide on the drop-down menu. The New Slide window (Figure 7.6) will reappear in the centre of the work area offering you a selection of layouts to choose from. Double click on the text only slide (Figure 7.6) and it will appear in the middle of your display.

7 Enter 'Syllabus' into the Add Title text box then in the Add Text box enter 'Seven modules' and it will appear as a bullet point. Press enter (return) to move to the next line and bullet point or click on the line below. Enter 'Module 1 – Underpinning Knowledge' and then on the next line 'Modules 2 to 7 – Practical'. Your slide should be similar to Figure 7.9.

Figure 7.8 First presentation

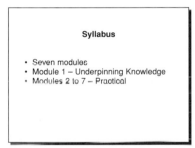

Figure 7.9 Second slide

8   The appearance of the slide can be changed using the options available on the Formatting toolbar (Figure 7.10). These are very similar to the options available in Word and Excel and are used in an identical way. First of all, click in the text box in order to activate it and then highlight the text you wish to change by clicking and holding down the left mouse button and dragging it over the area before releasing the button.

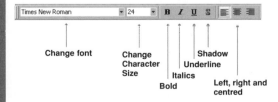

Figure 7.10 PowerPoint Formatting toolbar

9   Highlight the title and change its font, character size and embolden the text. Repeat the action with the other text box until you are content with the appearance of the slide. PowerPoint has an extra feature which is an automatic increase and decrease in the size of the text. These options are available on the Formatting toolbar (Figure 7.11).

Figure 7.11 Increase and decrease character size

10 The increase and decrease icon work in the same way as other options in that the text must be highlighted and then by clicking on either icon, you can see the size of the text increase and decrease. Explore the option until you are satisfied you can use it competently.

11 You have created a two-slide presentation. You can move between the two slides by using the scroll bar on the right edge of the work area. Do this.

12 To save the presentation, click on File on the menu bar and a drop-down menu will appear, click on Save and then the Save As window appears. This is identical to Figure 3.25 in Chapter 3 and the procedure for saving a presentation is the same. Name your file First Presentation and save it on to your floppy disk. If you want to update your presentation, you can save your overwritten file by clicking on Save again. Try this once you have saved First Presentation and you will notice that no Save As window opens. Microsoft Windows assumes you are saving it to the same location with the same name. If you need to change the location or name you need to use File menu item Save As.

13 You can save files in a variety of formats. The default is normally Presentation Document (i.e. .ppt) Other formats include:

(a) Presentation template

(b) Rich Text Format (.rtf)

(c) image file such as GIF or JPEG

(d) earlier versions of PowerPoint (e.g. 95, 3.0 and 4.0)

(e) HTML (i.e. suitable for posting to a website)

These formats allow the document to be read by other applications. A text or rich text file can be read by most word-processors. A template allows you to create new templates, HTML is a format suitable for the document to be posted to a website while PowerPoint 95/3.0/4.0 are earlier versions of the application. The normal process is that the latest version of the application will read earlier formats but an old version of PowerPoint will be unable to read a new format (e.g. PowerPoint 2000 will read all formats but PowerPoint 4.0 is unable to read PowerPoint 97 or PowerPoint 2000).

14 Practise your file saving by saving your file on to the floppy disk using a variety of formats. Since you have already saved the file once you need to use the File menu's Save As option. The Save As window will appear and if you click on the black triangle button next to Save as type box then a

drop-down list will appear of alternative formats. You select the new format by double clicking on it. A black triangle button always indicates a menu or list of other options.

Change the file name by adding a number (e.g. First Presentation 2 etc.) and the format to Rich Text Format, PowerPoint 4.0 and Presentation Template in turn. You may be presented with messages telling you that you may lose data by saving in this format but ignore them. Nevertheless in practice, by making a file readable for other applications you may change its format.

15 In order to save the presentation in HTML you need to use another function of the File menu which is Save as HTML.

16 Close First Presentation and Microsoft PowerPoint by using the window close button in top right-hand corner or use the Exit option in the File menu. If you have not saved the presentation since the last time you made a change, the application will warn you to save the file before closing the application.

TUTORIAL 7.2   Create a presentation

In addition to the standard layouts, PowerPoint provides you with many different presentation designs, standard presentations and help with web page layouts. These allow you rapidly to produce colourful and exciting sets of slides. If you click on File menu and then the New option the New Presentation window (Figure 7.12) appears giving you access to the many different design options. Figure 7.13 illustrates one of the presentation designs and standard presentation. The designs allow you to add the content you feel is appropriate to that design while the standard presentations offer suggestions of titles and content appropriate to a particular type of presentation.

PowerPoint also offers you the means to create a master text slide to control the presentation of text, colour and layout throughout your presentation. This is available through the View menu and Master option which provides access to the Slide Master. A master allows you to make changes to the whole presentation, while other means of applying changes to whole presentations are provided through the Format menu.

PowerPoint provides the means of cutting, copying, moving and deleting text in a similar way to other Microsoft office applications. However, the tools can also cut, copy, move and

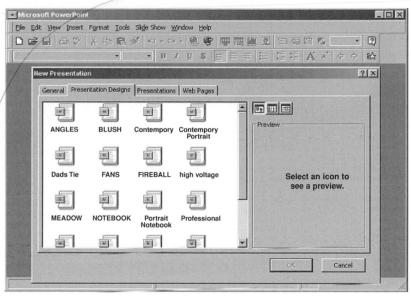

Figure 7.12 New Presentation

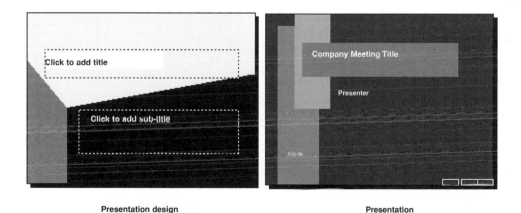

Presentation design

Presentation

Figure 7.13 Standard designs and presentations

delete images and whole slides. In all cases, the selected text, image or slide needs to be selected so that the application can recognise the chosen object. The tools are found within the Edit menu and on the Standard Toolbar. Figure 7.14 shows these functions and tools.

Text is selected by highlighting as it is in Word or Excel. Images are selected by clicking, which results in the image being enclosed in a box. This allows you to drag the illustration

around as well as cutting, copying and pasting it. In order to manipulate entire slides you need to view them in the slide sorter. This function is available in the View menu which also provides you with functions to list the contents of all the slides (i.e. Outline), add notes to each slide and run presentations. You can also create a master slide which provides you with a template for your whole presentation. All these functions can be seen in Figure 7.14.

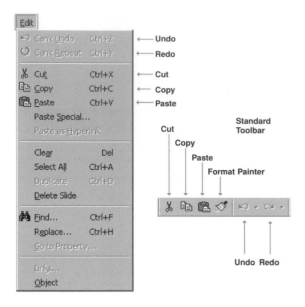

Figure 7.14 Cut, Copy and Paste

Slide sorter is launched by clicking on the View menu and then the Slide Sorter option which produces a display of all the slides as thumbnail images (Figure 7.15). These thumbnails are numbered in the order of the presentation and you can select individual slides by single clicking on your chosen slides which is then enclosed in a box. The slide can now be copied, cut and pasted or simply dragged and dropped using the mouse. To return to the individual slide view so that you can continue to design your presentation, you need to double click on your chosen one.

Although you are working with a variety of formats, it is possible to add extra text boxes to a slide or to enclose text in a box with a variety of line styles. These are available in the drawing toolbar shown in Figure 7.16. The toolbar provides access to a range of drawing and graphic tools some of which are similar to other Microsoft Office applications, for example changing the colour of the font or line. An important tool is the rotate function with which you can change the orientation of an image or object that you have created in your presentation.

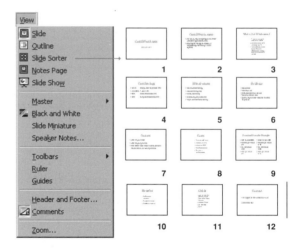

Figure 7.15 View Menu and Slide Sorter

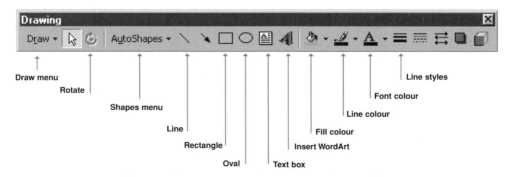

Figure 7.16 Drawing toolbar

Exercise 7.2

Create a new presentation

Duration 60 minutes

1   Load Microsoft PowerPoint.

2   Select Template and click OK and you will see the New Presentation template window with many thumbnails of standard presentations (Figure 7.12). If you single click on a choice you will see it displayed on the right of the window. Explore the choices until you identify a standard layout which will suit the making of a presentation to managers in your organisation then double click on the template. The standard layouts will appear for you to select an appropriate choice. You are going to present a case for all employees to have access to training leading to the ECDL qualification.

3   You should include in your presentation: higher productivity, motivation of staff and fewer mistakes. You need only develop about six slides and only create text slides. You will be using illustrations in your next exercise.

4   To insert a new slide you need to click on Insert menu and then on the option New Slide. The template appears with the standard layout window overlaying it for you to select the layout for the new one. This occurs each time that you insert a new slide. If you would like to move between slides then you can use the right-hand scroll bar to move forward and back.

5   During the creation of the presentation explore the options to change the line spacing, fonts and character sizes (see Tutorial 4.5). If you make a mistake remember the Undo and Redo on the standard toolbar and within the Edit menu.

6   You can change the style of the bullet points on the slide by highlighting the ones you would like to change and then selecting the Bullet option within the Format menu. This gives you a large selection of bullets from which to choose. Explore the different options.

7   You can also change the text by using the Format menu and the Font option. This provides you with the means of changing font, character size, adding shadow, superscript and subscript. Explore the different options.

8   Once you have created your short presentation then you can run the presentation by using the Slide Show option within the View menu or the short icon bar in the bottom left-hand corner of the application. These icons provide quick access to five useful functions. Figure 7.17 illustrates their purposes. These functions are also available in the View menu, as we have previously discussed.

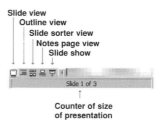

Figure 7.17 Icon bar

9   Use the five icons to run the slide show. You move from one slide to another by single clicking the mouse or pressing the space bar or enter key. When the show is completed you will return to the Slide View. Explore the five icons to see how quickly you can move between functions.

10 Use either the View menu option Slide Sorter or the icon bar Slide Sorter View to consider the overall view of your presentation. Copy one of your slides by clicking on it and using the copy option within the Edit menu or icon on standard toolbar and then paste the copy to another position within the presentation. You select a new position by clicking within the slides. This will insert a line showing the current position. The Paste option is located either in the Edit menu or standard toolbar icon.

11 Practise moving, copying and cutting slides within your presentation until you are satisfied you understand the techniques.

12 When you are developing a new presentation it is often useful to do so within the Slide Sorter so that you can easily change the order of the slides. Probably the most used function is Insert New Slide which can be achieved within a presentation by first selecting the location for new slide and then clicking on Insert menu and New Slide option. Practise inserting slides until you are competent.

13 To save the presentation click on File on the menu bar and a drop-down menu will appear, click on Save and the Save As window appears. Name your file Second Presentation and save it on to your floppy disk.

14 Close Second Presentation and Microsoft PowerPoint by using the window close button in the top right-hand corner or use the Exit option in the File menu.

Drawing

Duration 45 minutes

Exercise 7.3

1 Load Microsoft PowerPoint.

2 Select Blank Presentation and click OK. The standard layouts will appear. Choose the Title Only slide by double clicking on it (Figure 7.18). This will then appear in the work area.

Figure 7.18 Title Only slide

3 Add the drawing toolbar to your PowerPoint by clicking on View and then place your pointer on Toolbars so the list of optional toolbars appears. Click on Drawing, and the Drawing toolbar will appear. It can be in several forms depending on how you have used it previously. If it appears as a separate toolbar in the middle of the display, then drag it to the bottom or top of the display and it will automatically be incorporated into the application window.

4 You are now ready to use the drawing tools to fill the large area of empty space below the title but give your slide a title before you begin. Call it DRAWING using Ariel font and size 24 characters.

5 The Drawing toolbar provides you with a variety of tools (Figure 7.16) so explore them by placing different shapes on the slide. Figure 7.19 provides

you with an example, so try and replicate it. However, the purpose is to allow you to practise using the drawing tools. It is important to know how to use Rotate, use different types of lines, move lines around the slide, change attributes of a shape (e.g. colour), apply shadow, add colour and change objects.

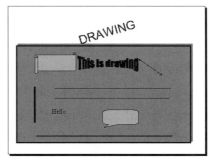

Figure 7.19 Example drawing

6 When you are confident that you understand the purpose of the drawing tools then save your slide. To save the presentation, click on File on the menu bar and a drop-down menu will appear, click on Save and the Save As window appears. Name your file Draw Presentation and save it on to your floppy disk.

7 Close Draw Presentation and Microsoft PowerPoint by using the window close button in the top right-hand corner or use Exit option in the File menu.

TUTORIAL 7.3 Graphics and other objects

Presentations are most effective if they capture the attention and interest of the audience. Illustrations are often useful for this. PowerPoint includes a large number of pictures which you can insert into your slides the same way that you place an image in a Word document. All Microsoft Applications has access to a picture bank (i.e. Microsoft Clip Gallery). Equally you can use images that you have screen captured, photographed with a digital camera, scanned into your computer or purchased. All are very helpful functions.

The standard layouts you can use to create presentations include a number that have areas designated for illustrations to be inserted. Alternatively, you can also choose to add an image to any slide using the option Picture in the Insert Menu. In both cases you will often use the resources provided by the Clip Gallery although the Picture options also lets you insert a picture stored in another file. Figure 7.20 shows the Insert Menu.

This menu also provides you with Object function which enables you to insert a wide variety of objects into your slides, including:

- Bitmap images
- Adobe Acrobat documents
- Lotus ScreenCam movies
- Excel worksheets
- Word documents

Other functions include Chart and Organisation Chart that you can use to create and then insert charts into your presentation. Less visual tools are Slide Number for inserting numbers on each slide to help you keep them in order and organise your presentation; and New Slide that inserts an additional one into your presentation at a point of your choosing.

Figure 7.21 illustrates Microsoft Clip Gallery. This is a library of clip art, digital pictures, sounds and videos that you can insert into Microsoft Office applications, including PowerPoint presentations. The contents of the Gallery can be extended using the Import Clips button. With this you can import resources stored elsewhere on your computer or on CD-ROMs or floppy disks. The Gallery resources are divided into several categories making them easy to find and enables you to add, delete and rename categories using the Edit Categories button.

When you select a category you can view its contents in the gallery. The image is selected by simply single clicking on it and the chosen images inserted by clicking on the Insert button.

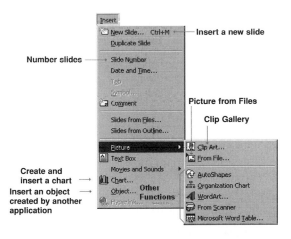

Figure 7.20 Insert menu

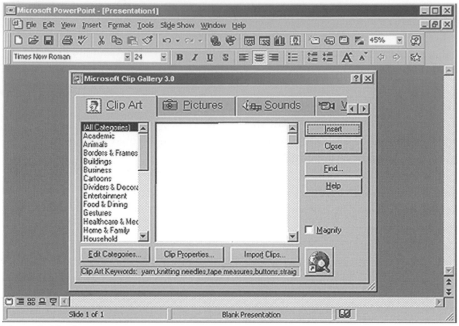

Figure 7.21 Microsoft Clip Gallery

Create an organisational chart

Duration 45 minutes

Exercise 7.4

1 Load Microsoft PowerPoint.

2 Select Blank Presentation and click OK. The standard layouts will appear. Choose the Organisation Chart option by double clicking on it (Figure 7.22). The slide shown in Figure 7.23 will appear. This slide instructs you to double click on it so follow the instructions and you will see a window entitled Microsoft Organisation Chart appear (Figure 7.24). This is an application for creating a chart using a drag and drop system. You select from the toolbars to add managers and subordinates.

Figure 7.22 Organisation Chart

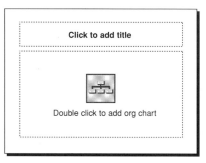

Figure 7.23 Organisation Chart slide

3 Create a small chart of part of your own organisation. Explore the system by considering each menu (e.g. Styles offers you additional features to produce an organisational chart). You insert the chart into your slide by clicking File menu and then Close and Return to Presentation. The first time you select this option, a message will appear asking you to confirm that you want to update the chart. Click on the Yes button.

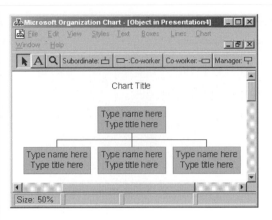

Figure 7.24 Creating an organisational chart

4 By clicking on the organisational chart you are able to make changes to it and so develop it in an iterative manner. If you make an error when you are using the Organisation Chart maker then help messages will appear to assist you.

5 Save your chart, click on File on the menu bar and a drop-down menu will appear, click on Save and the Save As window appears. Name your file Organisation Presentation and save it on to your floppy disk.

6 Close Organisation Presentation and Microsoft PowerPoint by using the window close button in the top right-hand corner or use the Exit option in the File menu.

PowerPoint also provides you with tools to include other forms of chart in your presentations. They operate in a similar way to the Organisation Chart tools. You select a slide layout which includes a chart (Figure 7.6). You have the option of a chart only slide or one which allows you to add text as well. You should explore this option since you can see how they look and then make subsequent changes to ensure your slides are well presented.

Using illustrations

Duration 45 minutes

1 Load Microsoft PowerPoint.

2 Select Blank Presentation and click OK. The standard layouts will appear. Choose one containing an image by double clicking on it (Figure 7.6). The slide shown in Figure 7.25 will appear. This instructs you to double click on it so follow the instruction and you will see a window entitled Microsoft Clip Gallery appear (Figure 7.21). This is an application which allows you to insert a graphic image.

Figure 7.25 Graphic Layout

3 Explore the different categories and options in Clip Gallery and select an image for your slide. When the image appears on your slide you will see that it is surrounded by a frame which allows you to change its size by clicking on one of the squares and holding down the left mouse button dragging the frame. You can make the image larger and smaller this way. Practise changing the size of the image and moving it around the slide. When you are finished, remove the frame by clicking elsewhere on the screen. If you want to manipulate the image later you can reinstate the frame by clicking on it.

4 If you want to add an image after you selected a slide layout you can do so by using the Insert Menu. You can do this with any slide so click on the Insert menu and then New Slide and standard layouts will appear. Chose a text-only slide by double clicking on it. The new slide will now appear in the work area of PowerPoint.

5 To add a picture, click on the Insert menu and then the place the mouse pointer on the Picture

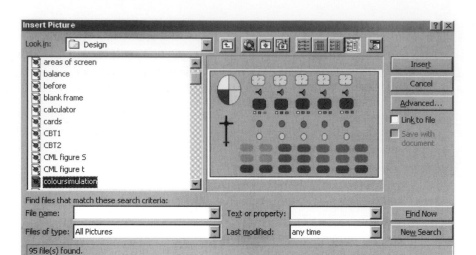

Figure 7.26 Inserting a picture from a file

option and a second menu will appear as shown in Figure 7.20. Click on Clip Art to access Microsoft Clip Gallery or From File if you have images stored elsewhere. In either case, once you have chosen a picture, double click or click on the Insert button to add it into your slide. Figure 7.26 illustrates the Insert Picture window when adding an image from a file. With this you can preview the picture prior to inserting it into your slide.

6 When the image appears it is enclosed in a frame. If you move your mouse pointer over the picture you will see the pointer change into a star. By holding down the left mouse button you can drag the image around the slide. By clicking on the squares in the frame and holding down the

left mouse button you can adjust the size of the image by dragging the frame. Try to move the image and change its size. Practise until you are confident.

7 In addition to inserting picture stored in files, you can import text, spreadsheets, a table and charts in the same way.

8 Save your image slide. Name your file Image Presentation and save it on to your floppy disk.

9 Close Image Presentation and Microsoft PowerPoint by using the window close button in the top right-hand corner or use the Exit option in the File menu.

TUTORIAL 7.4 Using your presentation

Once you have created your slide show you need to select how you are going to use it. PowerPoint provides you with a variety of choices. These include:

- on screen show;
- slide presentation;
- overhead projector slides;
- paper handouts;
- 35 mm slides.

However, before you start it is best to check that you have not made any spelling mistakes. It is too late noticing an error when you are in front of an audience. It is best to use the spell checker once you have created the presentation. The spell checker is located as an option Spelling in the Tools menu and works in the same way as it does within Word.

The slides are your visual aids but you usually need to prepare speaking notes as well and you can use PowerPoint to relate your notes to the slides. You can either click on the icon for Notes Page view in the bottom right-hand corner of the screen or click on View menu and then option Notes Page. Your slide will change to Figure 7.27. This provides you with an area for your notes under the slide. You can print the notes and slide one above the other by choosing Notes Page option in the print window. This is very useful in ensuring that your notes and slides are co-ordinated but you could also use this printout as a handout for your audience. An option which is often forgotten is the Outline View option. This is essentially a list of the content of the whole presentation which you can view on the screen (Outline option within View menu) or print out. There are a variety of other ways of printing slides to provide handouts and Figure 7.28 illustrates the range of options which are available to you through the Print window.

In addition to printing handouts and speaking notes, you can also print the slides as overhead transparencies. This requires that you load overhead transparency films into your printer. There are different types of films and you can seriously damage your printer if you use the wrong sort, so check the film specification before you load it.

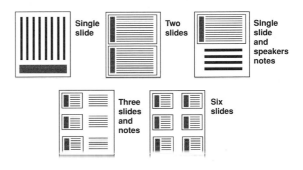

Figure 7.28 Printing options

Although all these different options of printing slides are provided, the two main ways of using PowerPoint presentations are on the screen. You can either develop a set of slides which are shown on the screen as a self-running presentation or one under your direct control (i.e. you select when you show each slide). Or, to make the slides more visible, the computer is frequently linked to a video projector so that an image can be projected on to a large screen. For a self-running presentation you can set the timings for each slide, having it visible for as long as you like. PowerPoint calls self-running presentations 'kiosk shows' and you can set them up using the Slide Show menu and Set Up Show option shown in Figure 7.29. To help run your presentations you can add on-screen navigation tools that are available in the Slide Show menu and the Action Buttons option which provides access to a number of choices.

Figure 7.27 Notes Page view

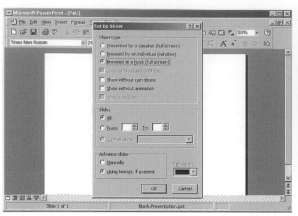

Figure 7.29 Set Up Show

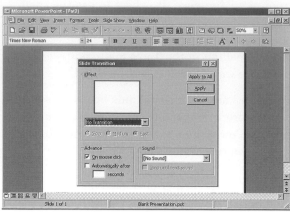

Figure 7.30 Slide Transition

PowerPoint provides you with a range of transition effects (i.e. different links between slides) available in Slide Show menu through the Slide Transition option. The Slide Show window (Figure 7.30) allows you to select from a list of transitions and also to try them out. You can have a standard transition throughout your presentation or a different link between each slide or any combination of these extremes. You can also set timings between slide changes and add sound effects.

As well as transitions, you can also add animation to your slides using the Slide Show Menu through the Preset Animation option which provides access to a list of animations. In order to use this function you need to select an object on a slide by clicking on it so that it is enclosed in its frame. You can then set the animations for each object. This can add considerable interest to a presentation but it is good practice to use animation and transitions only to gain your audience's attention and not to distract them with gimmicks. Animations

can be controlled by the speaker (i.e. by clicking the mouse) or be used automatically.

PowerPoint has several other options to aid your presentation. These include the following.

- Pack and Go Wizard – this helps you to compress and save your presentation on floppy disks and automatically collects all linked documents and resources so that you can easily transport your presentation to another computer.

- Two screen – you can connect two screens with a cable so that you are able to see your notes on one screen while the other is viewed by your audience.

- Custom shows – you can have multiple versions of the same presentation, each one customised to a particular audience.

- PowerPoint viewer allows you to show presentations on computers which do not have the PowerPoint application loaded on them.

Information and Communication Technologies (ICT)

By the end of this chapter you will be able to:

- open and close Microsoft Internet Explorer (a web browser);

- open and close Microsoft Outlook;

- understand the structure of the Web and an e-mail address;

- adjust toolbars and other settings of the applications;

- use a search engine;

- save a web page as a file and print a web page;

- bookmark a web page;

- create and send an e-mail message;

- read an e-mail message;

- attach a file to an e-mail;

- copy, cut, paste, move and delete text within an e-mail message and from other sources;

- open and save an attachment;

- use an address book;

- manage e-mail messages.

This chapter cover Module 6 of the ECDL syllabus. It is divided into tutorials which include exercises that will allow you to practise many of the concepts presented in the text. Each exercise indicates how long it should take you to complete. They can be undertaken anywhere you can gain access to a computer - work, college, a local library, learning centre or at home.

The tutorials in this chapter are as follows:

▶ TUTORIAL 8.1   What are Information and Communication Technologies (ICT)?

The World Wide Web provides access to millions of websites covering an immense range of subjects. The sites are provided by individuals, commercial companies, educational establishments, community groups, governments and many other people. There is considerable interest in using websites to sell products and services. It is possible to buy books, music, clothes, airline tickets, holidays and many other items. You can locate a hotel in another country and in some cases even book a room or visit the tourist information site to determine if you want to visit the area. However, many other sites simply offer information on a topic or have non-financial objectives (e.g. academic sites who want to disseminate the outcomes of their research). Some sites are essentially being used to provide information on a particular issue to change public opinion; help sufferers of illnesses or to bring together people with similar interests (e.g. football fans). Websites are very volatile and are changing and developing almost continuously. It is very common to return to a site to find that it is no longer available, has been completely changed or that it is out-of-date since no one has updated the information. This is essentially the information part of ICT.

The communication part of ICT for many Internet users is electronic mail or e-mail. This allows you to send messages to any other users with an e-mail account (equivalent to having an address) anywhere in the world at very low cost. The vast majority of Internet users quickly discover the value of e-mail and surveys of the Internet users show that over 95 per cent send and receive e-mail. There are many communication services based on e-mail including one known as mailgroups. A mailgroup provides the means of distributing a single e-mail message sent to a common address to all the members of the group. Some mailgroups have many thousands of members.

In order to access the information provided by the World Wide Web you need to use a software application called a browser and to send e-mail messages requires electronic mail

software. In both cases you must have registered with an Internet Service Provider (ISP) who connects your computer through a modem and a telephone line to the Internet through their machines. There are many different ISPs and many commercial companies offer free access to the Internet. However, this 'free' service is usually paid for through charges for telephoning help lines, telephone costs, advertising or a combination of these. Figure 8.1 illustrates a browser, Microsoft Internet Explorer 5.0, while Figure 8.2 illustrates the electronic mail application, Microsoft Outlook.

A browser looks similar to other Microsoft Office applications in that it has a title, menu and toolbars. These provide the detail functions available through the application. The next line is where you enter the website addresses which the browser uses to access the site. This only works after you have connected to the Internet. So the process is: connect to the Internet, launch your browser and then enter the address of the site you want to visit. If you are accessing the Internet through a company, college or learning centre network then the first step is probably hidden from you, meaning that you only have to launch your browser and enter the address.

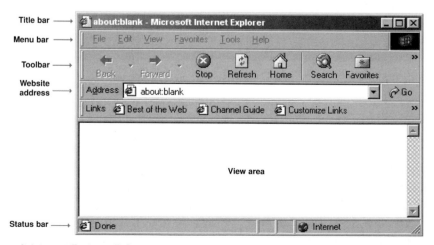

Figure 8.1 Microsoft Internet Explorer 5.0

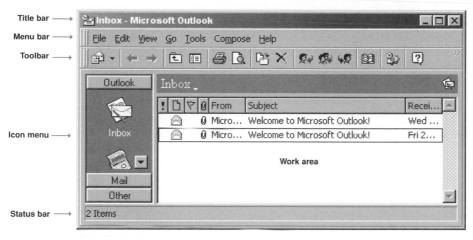

Title bar →
Menu bar →
Toolbar →
Icon menu →
Status bar →

Figure 8.2 Microsoft Outlook

Websites have unique addresses that are called a Uniform Resource Locator (URL) allowing you to locate the site and view its contents. A typical URL is http://www.example.co.uk. This is similar to a postal address – it describes the site in the same way an address describes the building. It shows you are seeking a World Wide Web site called 'example'. This is known as a domain name. The co.uk indicates that the site is a company in the United Kingdom. If you were to enter this URL into your browser, then you would be taken to the home page of this website.

A home page of a site can be compared to the contents page of a book. The home page is linked to the other pages which make up the site. Each page of a site has an individual address or URL so it is possible to jump directly to a particular site page. There is no need to visit the home page first. A page URL for our example site could be htttp://www.example.co.uk/thirditem/document.html. This shows you that you are accessing a page entitled document.html, which is linked to the home page via the page thirditem. Accurate site addresses are essential. The system can only locate your chosen addresses if it is perfectly correct.

Website addresses should show you both the type of organisation and country in which it is based if people follow the standard conventions. However, many organisations choose to ignore them and things are further complicated because a company in one country may choose to base its site in another. In Great Britain, many e-commerce businesses have adopted the prefix .com which should indicate that they are commercial businesses in the USA. However, in users' perception it has come to mean that it is an e-commerce business.

Some examples of standard features are given in Table 8.1.

URLs from the USA do not include a country code and so the absence of such a code indicates that it may be American.

The other key part of the address is the domain name. This is rather like the name of a company, organisation or person. Anyone can register domain names. If a website is hosted by another organisation then you will often see URLs with two domain addresses such as http://www.example.seconddomain.co.uk.

Type	Country		
.ac	University/academic	.ar	– Argentina
.com	Usually an American company	.ca	– Canada
.co	Business	.cu	– Cuba
.edu	Educational institution	.dk	– Denmark
.gov	Government	.eg	– Egypt
.int	International organisation	.fl	– Finland
.org	Charity	.gr	– Greece
.mil	Military	.hu	– Hungary
.net	Network related organisation	.ie	– Ireland

Table 8.1 Standard features of website addresses

Locating a website

Duration 30 minutes

Exercise 8.1

1 Launch Microsoft Explorer (assumes that the Internet link has already been established) by either double clicking on the Explorer icon on the Desktop or by clicking on Start, selecting Programs and then Microsoft Internet Explorer. Figure 8.1 shows the browser application in a window. If your computer displays the application in a window, expand it to fill the screen by using the maximise button in the top right-hand corner of the window.

2 Enter http://arnoldpublishers.com/geninfo/ Hodder.htm and press return. You will see a web page similar to that shown in the window in Figure 8.3. This is a home page and has links to other parts of the site. If you move your mouse pointer around the page it will change shape into a hand when it crosses a hyperlink. In this case, links are provided by a series of buttons down the left-hand side of the page. Other links are provided by small pictures or by underlined words.

3 Explore the site by clicking on any link you choose and seeing what it leads you to. In order to return

either seek out a link called home or click on the Back button on the browser toolbar. The Home link will take you straight back to the Home page while the Back button moves you back one page at a time.

4 Delete the address (URL) from the browser and enter one of the addresses below:

(a) www.bbc.co.uk (British Broadcasting Corporation)

(b) www.dfee.gov.uk (Department for Education and Employment)

(c) www.amazon.co.uk (Amazon online bookshop)

5 Explore the site of your choice in order to find out:

(a) what is the BBC's main educational initiative at the moment?

(b) what are the main aims of the Department for Education and Employment?

(c) what are the best-selling books?

6 Use the Back button on the browser toolbar and hyperlinks (use word, picture and button links) to

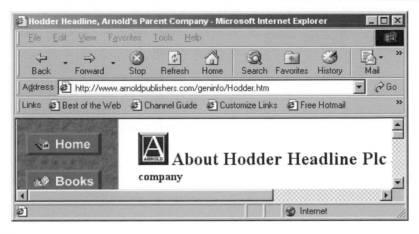

Figure 8.3 Web page

explore the sites and locate the required information. When you find web pages you would like to save then click on the File menu and Save or Save As options. This will open a window similar to those available in other Microsoft Office applications and working in the same way. You need to select the drive and folder in which to save the page as a file and name your file. Try this out with a page of your choice and save it as a file to your floppy disk. The alternative to capturing web pages as a file is to print the contents. Print your chosen page by clicking on File menu and then Print which opens the Print window which allows you to choose from a variety of options. On this occasion simply click on the OK button in Print window.

7 When you want to close the browser click on the File menu item and an option on the drop-down menu is Close which, if clicked, will close the browser. Another way of closing the browser is to click on Close window in the right-hand corner. In both cases you can close the browser no matter where you are in the site.

TUTORIAL 8.2 Adjust your browser

You can adjust your browser using the Internet Options window which can be accessed from Internet Explorer Tools menu or from Control Panel within Settings. Control Panel is accessed by clicking on Start to and by placing pointer on Settings option that reveals a menu with Control Panel. By clicking on Control Panel you will see many different options for controlling the computer system. Figure 8.4 shows the icon, which, by double clicking, you access Internet Options (Figure 8.6).

The other way of changing the browser settings is from within Internet Explorer. The Tools menu (Figure 8.5) contains the option Internet Options. By clicking on this option opens Internet Options (Figure 8.6). This way is probably preferable when you are in the process of searching the Internet while the Control Panel is available to set your browser prior to accessing the Internet.

Figure 8.4 Internet Options icon

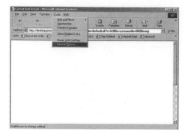

Figure 8.5 Internet Explorer Tools menu

Figure 8.6 shows Internet Options. You will notice that it is divided into several different sections using a range of tabs (e.g. General, Security, Content, Connections, Programs and Advanced). We will only consider General and Advanced. The General page covers three main choices – Home Page, Temporary Internet Files and History. The Home Page option lets you choose a website that you can automatically go to every time you connect to the Internet. The default setting is usually your Internet Service Provider, company or college site if you are using their systems to access to the Internet. However, you can enter the address of another site or simply choose not to connect to any site

automatically. Using Internet Options you either enter the URL of your choice or leave it blank.

Temporary Internet files are web pages and images are copied to this folder in order to speed up access to the websites. Many users are not aware they are being stored. Internet Options allows you to set the size of the folder and hence how many temporary files are held, how they are updated and deleted. It is essentially a housekeeping package but very useful in balancing whether you have your computer with many hundreds of megabytes of Internet files or slower access to the websites you frequently visit.

The third set of options concern the History records which essentially keep a record of sites visited. This is very useful if you want to revisit a site but have forgotten its address. You need to set how many days of records to keep. You can select from 0 to many hundreds of days but you should consider a balance between a useful record which allows you to retrace your steps and an enormous record file.

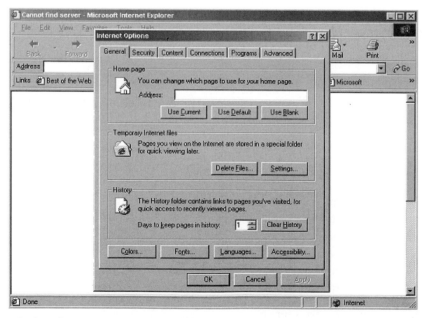

Figure 8.6 Internet Options 1

The Advanced tab (Figure 8.7) reveals a long list of options which you select using the mouse pointer. You will see that options that are selected (e.g. Show pictures) have a tick in their box. If you click on a ticked box it will be de-selected and if you click on an empty box it will be selected. The effect of de-selecting Show pictures means that websites will show you their text but not their pictures. This will speed up access since it reduces the size of the pages but, of course, it does limit the information on each page.

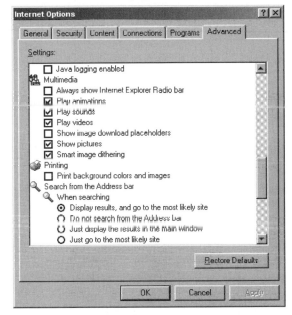

Figure 8.7 Internet Options 2

Microsoft Internet Explorer offers you a Help function which is very similar to other Microsoft Office applications. It is accessed and used in the same way. Tutorial 4.2 is provided on the Help function in Chapter 4 so by understanding how to use Help in Microsoft Word you will be able to use the function in Internet Explorer. The Help function is located on the menu bar of the applications. If you click on the Internet Explorer Help menu item then Figure 8.8 will appear. If you click on the Contents and Index option you will be

presented with a list of the contents of the Help function. You can search the list by entering a word in the top box.

Figure 8.8 Internet Explorer Help menu

A key feature of many Microsoft applications are the toolbars which provide extra functionality. With Internet Explorer, you can customise your toolbars in a similar way to other Microsoft applications. Figure 8.9 shows the Standard, Address and Links toolbars.

To change a toolbar you need to click on the View menu option which reveals a drop-down menu containing the option Toolbars. If you click on Toolbars then a short list of possible toolbars are provided. Figure 8.9 indicates that the Standard, Address and Links toolbars have been selected since a tick is displayed alongside the option. A toolbar can be removed by clicking on the options and the tick and toolbar will be removed. This method of changing toolbars is, of course, identical to all Microsoft Office applications.

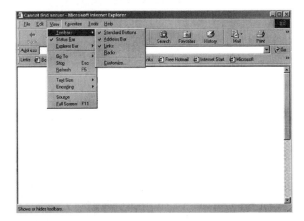

Figure 8.9 Toolbar

The richness and scope of the millions of websites available to you, and covering almost every conceivable subject, causes the greatest problem in using the Web. How do you locate sites related to your chosen subject? The answer is to use what are called search engines. These are specialist sites that provide a location service for you at no charge.

Search engines work by trying to match keywords that you enter with the contents of sites around the Web. Figure 8.10 shows the search engine, Chubba (http://www.chubba.com/) which is actually a means of searching five other search engines (Alta Vista, Kanoodle, Infoseek and GoTo and Lycos) with a single survey.

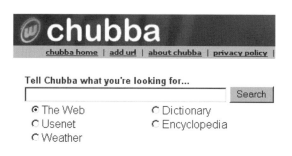

Figure 8.10 Chubba search engine

All search engines work in a similar way. When you enter some keywords and click on Search, the engine will rapidly produce a list of web pages which match the keywords either in the text or in the title of the page. Often, the search will report matches with very large numbers of pages sometimes even in the millions. The search engine will list them in the order it thinks are the closest matches to your keywords. This is a very fast process since the engine is not searching the Web but its own database which is continuously updated

by searching the actual web pages. This is done by using a software tool which is sometimes called a spider. It is important to realise that the engines are reporting pages not sites and so will often list many pages from a single site. Although the engine will report large numbers of matches it will normal only show you 10 or 20 of them at any one time and indicate the degree of match (e.g. 90%) so you can quickly check if your search has been successful. A problem which many search engines face is the rapid growth of the Web which makes it difficult for them to keep up to date.

There are many search engines. You need to explore them to identify those that meet your needs. Some examples are:

AltaVista	http://www.altavista.digital.com/
Chubba	http://www.chubba.com/
Dogpile	hhtp://.www.dogpile.com/
Excite	http://www.excite.com/
Google	http://www.google.com/
Gutterrat	http://www.gutterrat.com/
HotBot	http://www.hotbot.com/
Infoseek	http://www.infoseek.com/
Looksmart	http://www.looksmart.com/
Lycos	http://www-uk.lycos.com/
Magellan	http://www.mckinley.com/
Northern Lights	http://www.nlsearch.com/
Webcrawler	http://www.webcrawler.com/

Search engines can also be used to find newsgroup messages and individual e-mail addresses. There are several that specialise in locating e-mail addresses.

Bigfoot   http://www.bigfoot.com/

Four11   http://www.Four11.com/

InfoSpace   http://www.www.infospace.com/

Whowhere   http://www.whowhere.com/

Yahoo People   http://people.yahoo.com/

Other search engines offer to answer questions. These include:

Ask Jeeves   http://www.ask.com/

Answers   http://www.answer.com/

Electronic Library   http://www.elibrary.com/

Information Please   http://www.infoplease.com/

Searching using keywords may seem a very simple process but it is important to understand how your words are treated. Most search engines offer a help function, tips or advanced search ideas. It is useful to explore these options as they will assist you in locating the pages you are seeking. Some useful tips for using search engines are:

1. Entering several words means that the engine hunts for pages which contain each word but in the order you have entered them. So the keywords **French villas** means that the engine seeks pages containing the word **French** before seeking pages with the word **villas**.

2. If you enclose your key words in inverted commas, "**French villas**" then the search is for pages containing that exact phrase but will ignore sites containing only one of these words.

3. Using capital letters will locate those pages containing words in capitals and this may limit the pages located.

4. You can use the + and – signs to include or exclude words. If we search for **french+villas** then the search will be for pages containing the word French and also villas. A minus sign such as **French–villas** means it will locate pages with the word **French** but not containing the word **villas**.

5. It is also possible to search using logical operators AND, OR and NOT. These allow the construction of complex searchers. For example **French AND villas NOT** houses means a search for **French** pages with the word **villas** but not the word **houses**. Other examples are:

   ◢ **French AND villas OR houses** – **French** pages with either words **villas** or **houses**

   ◢ **French OR Spanish** – pages containing the word **French** or **Spanish**

All search engines work in different ways so it is important to explore them to determine which ones best meet your needs.

Many websites (including search engines) offer a directory service which is essentially a large number of web pages organised into categories. These help you to locate useful websites if you are interested in one or more of the categories. Directories have the considerable advantage that entries have been selected so that you are not normally faced with thousands of hits to look through.

Set your browser and search for a site

Duration 60 minutes

Exercise 8.2

1 Launch Microsoft Explorer (assumes that Internet link has already been established) by either double clicking on the Internet Explorer icon on the Desktop or by clicking on Start, selecting Programs and then clicking on Microsoft Explorer.

2 Using the Internet Options function within the Tools menu (Figure 8.5) explore changing your browser settings (e.g. by checking or unchecking Show pictures). This is best achieved by making a change and then accessing a website – then reversing the change and accessing the same website. You will be able to compare the speed of access and the appearance of the site with and without pictures. Continue this process until you are confident that you understand.

3 Choose one of the search engines discussed earlier and enter its URL into the address box of the Internet Explorer browser and press Enter. When the engine has loaded try searching for a house, apartment or villa to rent for a holiday in France. Try a number of search queries such as:

(a) **France house apartment villa**

(b) **France AND house OR apartment OR villa**

(c) **"France house apartment villa"**

(d) **France+house**

(e) **France+apartment**

(f) **France+villa**

4 Compare the different results and experiment with other search queries until you understand the most effective type of search.

5 Use the search engine's help, tips and advanced searching functions if it has them to learn more about searching with that engine.

6 Select different search engines and repeat the searches that you found most effective to see if you can identify any differences in performance between the engines.

7 Continue until you are satisfied.

8 When you find a web page which is helpful with your search for a holiday home then you can use it to practise saving and printing it. To save a page, click on the File menu and Save or Save As options. This will open a window similar to those available in other Microsoft Office applications and which works in the same way. You need to select the drive and folder in which to save the page as a file and name your file. Save the page as a file to your floppy disk. Practise printing your selected page by clicking on File menu and then Print which opens the Print window so you can choose from a variety of options. On this occasion simply click on the OK button in the Print window. A printout of your chosen page will result.

9 When you have finished, close the browser either by using the Close option in the File menu or click on the close button in the top right-hand corner of the window. This closes the browser but your link with the Internet may still be open and closing it depends on your ISP and the location from which you are accessing the Internet (e.g. your company or a college). Most companies and colleges will not require you to close the link since it is part of the whole organisation network.

TUTORIAL 8.4 Bookmarks

The World Wide Web offers you enormous opportunities to locate new information relating to almost any subject. This does present the problem of remembering where the websites are and how to find them again. Internet Explorer provides a facility to mark sites so that you can return to them by simply clicking on the bookmark. In Internet Explorer the bookmarks are called Favorites and you can make a site a Favorite by simply clicking on the Favorite menu item and then on Add to Favorites option. This lets you create a list of Favorite locations.

Obviously your list will become extensive so the function helps you organise the list into folders. Figure 8.11 illustrates my Favorite folders. Accessing the Organize Favorites option through the Favorites menu helps you to create new folders as well as to move Favorites around.

The folders are stored in the Favorite menu and by locating the site you want to visit and clicking on it, you will be taken directly to it. This is very useful and effective.

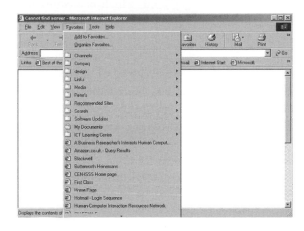

Figure 8.11 Favorites

TUTORIAL 8.5 E-mail

E-mail is a vital part of communication technology and has had a significant impact on communication. E-mail is a worldwide electronic postal service and most Internet Service Providers (ISP) give you an e-mail account as part of providing you with access to the Internet. Many websites provide free e-mail servers to anyone who can gain access to the Internet so that it is perfectly possible to use e-mail through public access such as local cybercafes. You can have several accounts for yourself and your family. Many people will have a personal account, a work account and a hobby account. However, this depends on your contract with the provider, employer or college. E-mail is:

 low cost (i.e. a very short telephone call);

very fast (i.e. a few minutes to travel thousands of miles);

not limited to text (e.g. pictures, sounds and video can be attached to an e-mail);

not restricted by time; you can send a message any time you like;

you can send one message to as many people as you want.

E-mail is similar to surface mail in that you must follow a standard agreed method of use. E-mail requires:

an address;

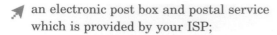 an electronic post box and postal service which is provided by your ISP;

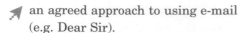 an agreed approach to using e-mail (e.g. Dear Sir).

A typical e-mail address is peter@friend.co.uk. This tells you the person's username is peter, his domain name is friend, which is a company (co) based in the United Kingdom (uk). This is a typical address of a person working in a business. If you are sending a message to an individual then they may have an address showing you the name of their ISP such as peter@isp.co.uk or peter@brown.isp.co.uk. The ISP's name is substituted for isp in this example. In the latter case the ISP allows their customers to have their own domain name (i.e. brown) which is added to the address.

E-mail addresses are similar to postal addresses in that they indicate who you are sending mail to and where they are. An e-mail address indicates, through codes, the type of organisation (e.g. .com – a commercial company, probably in the USA) and in which country they are based (e.g. .cu – Cuba). It is very important to be precise with e-mail addresses. You cannot rely on a local postman or woman recognising the mistake and still delivering the mail to the right person. Computers can only work with correct addresses. If your e-mail is not delivered then you will probably get an error message. The main reason for non-delivery is an incorrect address but it is also sometimes due to problems with the recipient's computer or ISP's server.

Figure 8.2 shows the Microsoft Outlook Inbox which is essentially a mail tray for your electronic mail. It provides you with a list of messages you have received, giving the basic information of the sender, the subject of the message and the date it was sent. It also uses a variety of symbols to indicate the status of

the message so that a closed envelope indicates that the message has not been opened while an open envelope (see Figure 8.2) shows that the message has been read. Other symbols include:

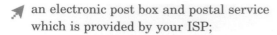 a paperclip indicating an attached file;

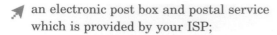 an exclamation mark showing a message is urgent;

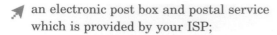 a down arrow indicating a message of low importance.

You can view a message by double clicking on it and the message appears in a window (Figure 8.12). The alternative to double clicking is that you can highlight a message and use the Open option within the File menu. The highlight bar can be moved by single clicking or by using the keyboard arrow keys. When a message is highlighted you can save it to a folder of your choice by using the Save or Save As options in the File menu. Alternatively you could use the copy or cut and paste options to move messages to folders. This is important since you will rapidly be receiving many e-mails and you need to consider how to organise them into a series of folders so that you can find them again. This requires you to save the messages with names you can easily remember within folders and then group the messages under common themes. To remove a message from the Inbox is important since quickly you can have a list of hundreds of e-mails if you do not delete your old messages. You can delete a message simply by highlighting and pressing the delete key.

Figure 8.12 shows a Microsoft Outlook Message window. This is opened by selecting the New option in the File menu. This provides a range of options including Mail Message which will open the Message window if clicked. This is the area in which you write and address your message. You can send your message directly to multiple addresses or copy it to other people. It is possible to create a standard list so that rather than having to enter many individual addresses you can simply enter a single item. This is very useful in an organisation, enabling distribution lists for different types of messages to be developed. An extra feature of a message is a blind copy. This is the ability to send a copy to a person without the other recipients knowing you have sent them a copy. This is available within the View menu as the Bcc Field option but only within the Message window toolbar. When the option is selected the message window (Figure 8.12) changes to include an extra blind copy line below the Cc line. This allows you to enter addresses to which you want to send blind copies. A final useful feature of e-mail is that you can attach files to the message from other applications (e.g. Word files). These are opened by double clicking on the attachment. The file is opened within its appropriate application. However, if you receive a file for an application that you do not own then you will not be able to read it. If the file opens, you can save it in the normal way.

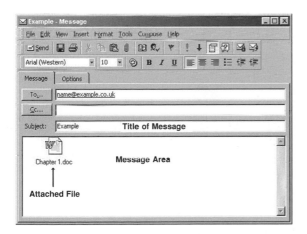

Figure 8.12 Microsoft Outlook Message window

Internet e-mail was designed to send text-only messages. In order to attach files they need to be encoded as text and there are two main ways of doing this in Windows – Multipurpose

Internet Mail Extensions (MIME) and Uuencoding. It is a frequent experience to be told by recipient of your e-mail that they cannot open your attachments. This is caused either by the encoding or by the fact that the file is incompatible with their applications. It is sensible to explain within the e-mail, the type of attachment you have enclosed.

Figure 8.13 shows a message you might receive. You should notice that it tells you who has sent the message and the date and time it was sent. E-mail messages tend to be short but there is no limit on how long the message could be. However, normal practice is to send long messages in the form of a Word file attached to the e-mail.

Outlook provides you with an auto-signature facility that enables you to add a standard message automatically to the end of all your e-mails. This could simply be your name but many people customise their e-mails to reflect personal interests. This facility is available as an option within the Tools menu called Autosignature.

In common with all Microsoft applications, Outlook has a Help function, similar to other Microsoft Office applications. It is accessed and used in the same way. A tutorial on the Help function is provided in Chapter 4.

Figure 8.13 Receiving a message

The Help function is located on the menu bar of the applications. If you click on the Outlook Help menu item then Figure 8.14 will appear. If you click on the Contents and Index option you will be presented with a list of the contents of the Help function. You can search the list by entering a word in the top box.

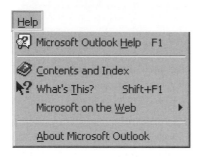

Figure 8.14 Microsoft Outlook Help

Microsoft Outlook can be set to work either offline or online, that is, you can write and reply to e-mails whether you are connected to the Internet or not. If you compose messages while offline, they are not sent until you next connect to the Internet. If you are using a company or college network then offline working is relatively unimportant since the network is permanently linked to the Internet, but it is useful if you connect over a telephone link since you do not incur telephone charges while you are writing your messages, only when you send them. If you would like to explore this option use the Help system to explain how to set Outlook for offline working.

Sending and receiving messages

Duration 60 minutes

Exercise 8.3

1 Launch Microsoft Outlook either by double clicking on the Outlook icon on the Desktop or by clicking on Start, selecting Programs and then Microsoft Outlook. Figure 8.2 shows Outlook in a window. If your computer displays the application in a window, expand it to fill the screen by using the maximise button in the top right-hand corner of the window.

2 On the left-hand side of the application is a series of icons which open different functions within Outlook. Explore the options by single clicking on the icons and return to the Inbox. Figure 8.15 illustrates three icons. You can add new folders to this list using the New option within File menu. This opens a menu with the option Folder in which you can name your new folder. The obvious use of a new folder is to sort messages received. Create a new folder called Messages and practise moving e-mails that you have received into it using copy and paste.

Figure 8.15 Outlook icons

3 The view of all the Outlook functions can be changed and adjusted to suit your precise needs. The changes are made using the options available within the View menu (Figure 8.16). Explore the different options including the Sort option which is illustrated in Figure 8.17. The View menu also provides you with a choice of Toolbars in the same way as other Microsoft applications but only two toolbars are available for the Inbox function. Figure 8.16 shows the Standard toolbar. The

additional toolbar is called Remote which can help you connect to a remote mail service. When you have finished your explorations then return the display to the Inbox. In different functions there are different toolbar options but accessed in an identical way.

4 The most important functions are obviously sending and receiving e-mails so the next step is to create an e-mail. This can be a reply to a message you have been sent or a new message. If you have a message in your Inbox then let's reply to it. Double click on the message to open the message window.

Figure 8.16 Outlook View menu

5 Figure 8.13 shows you a message. Notice that the Standard toolbar contains three buttons for replying. These are Reply, Reply to All and Forward. The Reply option allows you to send a message to the individual who sent the original message while Reply to All provides you with the means of responding not only to the person who sent the message, but to everyone else included in the original message. Forward is the function which allows you to share the original message with other people.

6 Click on Reply and you will see a duplicate Message Window appear and then change to fill the address box with the address of the sender

and add Re. to the subject. The original message is moved down the message area to clear a space for your reply (Figure 8.18). This is very useful because your response and original message are combined in a single e-mail. It is normal to carry out a conversation with a complete record being held on the e-mail.

7 Add a reply to the message and when you have finished click on the Send button on the toolbar of the message window. You will see your message posted in that it disappears and you are returned to the original message. You can close the message by clicking on the close icon in the right-hand corner of the window or use the File menu option Close. You can reply without returning the original message by simply noting the sender's e-mail address and creating a new message.

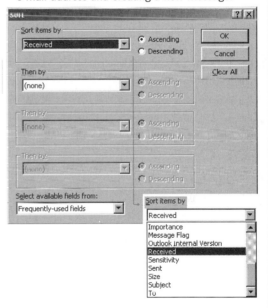

Figure 8.17 Outlook View Sort option

8 The Reply to All option works in an identical way except you see all the people who received the original message being sent the reply (i.e. appearing in the address box). The Forward option is different in that you have to insert the address of the person you want to copy the original message to and you can add a message

to explain why you are forwarding the information. Explore these options until you have identified the similarities and differences.

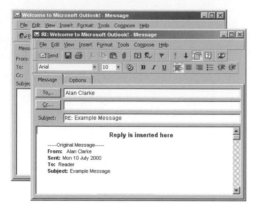

Figure 8.18 Reply to an e-mail

9 The Inbox icon bar contains a button called Mail. Click on this button and the bar will change to show four icons (i.e. Inbox, Sent Items, Out Box and Deleted Items). If click on Sent Items the display of items will change to reveal a list of the messages you have sent. You can read them by double clicking on them. The Outbox icon links you to a list of e-mails waiting to be sent, that is, messages prepared offline which will be sent next time you connect to the Internet. The Deleted Items provides access to messages you have deleted so that you can restore them if you have made a mistake. You can move between these functions by single clicking on the icons. Explore the functions.

10 Sending a new e-mail is very similar to replying to a message. You single click on the File menu and then place your pointer on New to reveal a new menu where you need to click on Mail Message (Figure 8.19) and this will open a blank message window which is identical to Figure 8.13 except with boxes and the message area empty. You now need to enter an address. This can be a friend, colleague or another student. You access the address box by clicking in it. You move to the subject by clicking in that box. Enter Test in the

subject box. Next enter the message below, again by initially clicking in the message area.

Hello

This is a test e-mail. Could you reply to me so that I can see what happens?

Many Thanks

You are now going to add an autosignature by clicking on the Tools menu and the Autosignature option which produces a wide window shown in Figure 8.20. You enter your message which will be added to the bottom of all your e-mails and click on the radio button – add this signature to the end of new messages. The function allows you to select a font and justify the text (Paragraph button). When you have completed your Autosignature, you can insert it by clicking on the Insert button. You will see your message appear in the e-mail.

Figure 8.19 New e-mail message

11 You could now send the message by clicking on the Send button on the toolbar but first we will attach a file to the message. This is achieved by single clicking on the Insert menu and then on the File option. This opens the folder structure so that you can search your files and folders for a file to

Figure 8.20 Autosignature function

insert. You can also change your drive to alter the Look In: box to show your Floppy Disk drive and select one of the files you have created in another Microsoft Office application. To attach a file, simply double click on the file and you will see it appear in your message. Obviously this file is not relevant to your message so we should remove it. To delete the file, single click on it and you will see it enclosed in a rectangle showing you that it is highlighted. Press the delete button on the keyboard and the file will be removed. If you double click the file by error, you will open the attached file. You can return by simply closing the open application. This can be useful for checking that you are adding the correct file.

12 Practise adding and removing files to your message until you are confident that you understand the process.

13 You are now ready to send a file. Before sending your e-mail, check your spelling by clicking on the Tools menu and the option Spelling. This will open the spelling function which is similar to that available in other Microsoft applications. Try it out on your short message.

14 You can send a message with different degrees of priority. You access these choices by clicking on icons on the toolbar (Figure 8.21) or clicking on the Options tab (Figure 8.22).

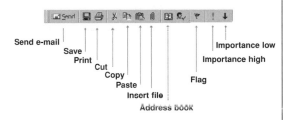

Figure 8.21 Some toolbar icons

15 You can set the degree of importance by single clicking either of the importance icons or neither of them which leaves the degree of importance as normal. The other option is the Flag which provides you with the means of sending messages to explain the nature of the e-mail. The Options window also allows the sensitivity of the message to be set (e.g. normal, personal, private and confidential). Explore these choices to see what is available.

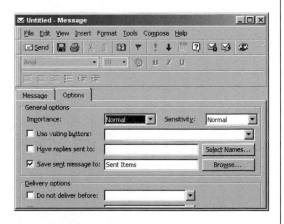

Figure 8.22 Outlook Options

16 The icons provide you with other tools similar to other Microsoft Office applications. These include Cut, Copy and Paste. You can cut, copy and paste within a message and between messages or from and to other Microsoft applications such as Word and Excel. It is often useful to copy an e-mail message to a Word document.

17 Within a message you have the basic functions available in Word to embold text, select different

fonts and character sizes, select different font colours and justify your text. It is a limited word-processor.

18 Explore these different features and when you are ready, send your message.

19 Close the application either by using the Tools menu and either options E̲xit or Exit and L̲og Off or otherwise close the window using the close window button in the top right-hand corner.

TUTORIAL 8.6 Organising your e-mails

When you are using e-mails regularly, you will probably discover that you are both receiving and sending far more than you originally expected. Many e-mail users send and receive scores of messages each day. It is therefore important to organise them. Most e-mail systems provide you with an electronic address book to keep individual records and also to help you create distribution lists. Microsoft Outlook provides an address book which is accessed through the T̲ools menu and the Address B̲ook option or by clicking on the address book icon (Figure 8.21). Figure 8.23 shows the Address Book.

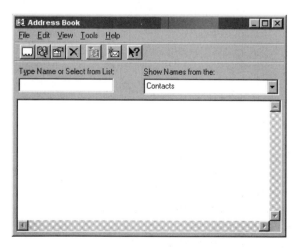

Figure 8.23 Outlook Address Book

The other form of address records is the Contacts folder (Figure 8.24) in which detailed information such as addresses, telephone and fax numbers about individual people can be kept as well as e-mail addresses. Contacts where the e-mail address is completed are automatically included in the Outlook Address Book. There are several different types of address book including the following.

- Global Address List – this normally holds all the addresses for individuals, groups and distribution lists in your organisation to whom you can send e-mails. It is established by the network system administrator so that if you are working on a standalone computer it is probably not relevant to you.

- Outlook Address Book – this is created from the contact records.

- Personal Address Book – this is intended to store your private addresses.

The most straightforward way of adding a new address to the Contacts folder is from a message you have received. This is achieved by opening the message and positioning the mouse pointer over the address then clicking the right mouse pointer. Figure 8.25 illustrates

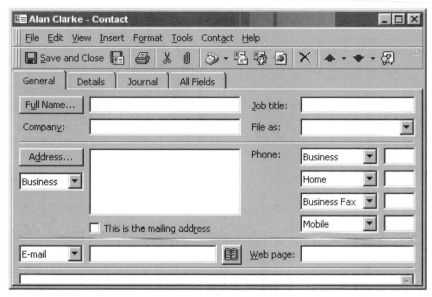

Figure 8.24 Outlook Contacts

the method. The menu which appears has the option A̲dd to Contacts that allows you to add the messages e-mail address to the Contacts folder.

In both cases, you complete the information you know and leave the rest blank. There is a large area at the bottom of the form for you to add notes.

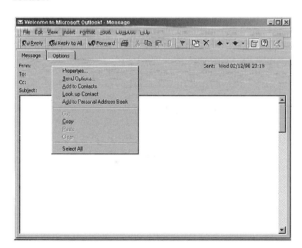

Figure 8.25 Adding an address to the Contact Folder

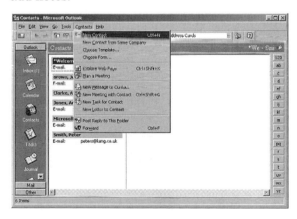

Figure 8.26 Contacts menu

The other method is to move into the Contacts function by clicking on the Contacts icon. The Contacts Menu bar has a C̲ontacts Menu item (Figure 8.26) which in turn has a N̲ew Contact option. This will open a blank contacts form for you to complete manually.

A personal address list is a means of sending an e-mail to a group of people by simply selecting a list name. You create a list by clicking on T̲ools menu and selecting the Address B̲ook option (Figure 8.27). However, this does assume that you have set up your user profile to accept a personal address book.

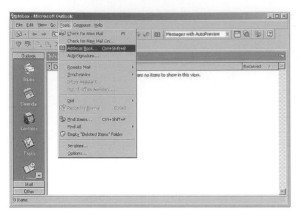

Figure 8.27 Selecting Address Book

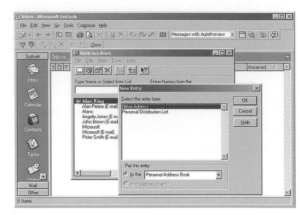

Figure 8.28 Services window

This is undertaken by using the Service option within the Tools menu. Figure 8.28 illustrates the Services window.

When you select the Address Book option then the window shown in Figure 8.23 is opened. This allows you to select the personal address book option and then new entry. This will open the window shown in Figure 8.29. In this window you can create a distribution list. Your lists can be extended or amended at any time

through these options. There is no limit to the number of lists you can create and in many organisations individual users are provided with some standard distribution lists. These often include the management group, team lists, sales staff and other lists determined by work relationships. Whole organisation lists are obviously useful to send everyone messages without having to enter many separate addresses.

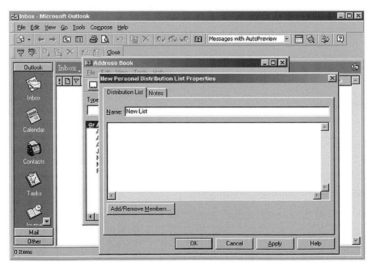

Figure 8.29 New Personal Distribution List Properties window

Glossary

Analogue:	This is continuous data as opposed to discrete information or digital data
Application software:	This is a program designed to perform a task such as designing a database, completing a spreadsheet or word-processing
Baud:	A measure of the transmission rate of information
Boot:	This is the process of starting up a computer and involves the loading of the operating system and checking the hardware
Browser:	A browser is an application which allows you to access a World Wide Web site
Bps (bits per second):	A bit is the smallest unit of information (i.e. 1 or 0) that can be used by a computer or sent across a communication link. Bits per second are often the measure of the flow of information
Byte	This is a measure of memory and is sufficient memory to store a single character (e.g. a number or letter)
CAD	see **Computer Aided Design**
CD-R:	Compact Disk Recordable allows you to record information to a compact disk once only
CD-ROM:	Compact Disk – Read Only Memory is the computer equivalent of an audio compact disk and is used to store large amounts of information. You can read information from a CD-ROM but you cannot record information on to the disk
CD-RW:	Compact Disk Read Write allows you to record and erase information from a compact disk
Chipset:	A set of silicon chips which serves to provide the computer with particular features (e.g. control of video)
Client Server	see **server**
Computer Aided Design:	A special application which assists you to design objects and systems (e.g. engineering components)
CPU	see **Central Processing Unit**
Central Processing Unit:	This is the silicon chip which controls the operation of the computer
Desktop Publishing:	A special application which allows you to design publications such as newsletters and papers
Digital:	Digital information is made up of patterns of noughts and ones
Domain:	The domain is part of a website or e-mail address. It shows the type of organisation hosting the site (e.g. www.fred.co.uk fred is the domain)
DOS:	This is an operating system called the Disk Operating System
DTP	see **desktop publishing**
Dumb terminal:	This is a monitor and keyboard which is connected to a main frame or mini-computer. It has no local processing power and is therefore deemed to be dumb

DVD:	Digital Video Disk is a new form of disk resembling a CD-ROM but able to hold considerably more material
DVD drive:	Digital Video Disk is a new form of compact disk which allows huge amounts of information to be stored on a disk so that a single disk can store the contents of an entire movie
DVD RAM:	Digital Video Disk Random Access Memory allows you to record and erase information from a DVD
ECDL	see **European Computer Driving Licence**
E-commerce	see **Electronic Commerce**
Electronic commerce:	This is the term for using the World Wide Web to promote your business through marketing, direct selling or communicating with customers
E-mail	see **Electronic mail**
Electronic mail:	This is both the process of sending a message through the Internet; and the name of the message
European Computer Driving Licence:	The European Computer Driving Licence (ECDL) is a qualification which is accepted across Europe and North America
Expansion slot:	This is an empty slot within the computer which allows you to insert extra electronic boards to extend the capability of the computer
Fax:	This is a hardware system which allows you to copy and send documents between fax machines linked by a telephone line
GUI	see **Graphical User Interface**
Graphical User Interface:	This is a type of interface display which combines icons, windows and a mouse pointer to produce an easy-to-use environment
Hard disk:	the computer's internal magnetic disk on which a large amount of information can be stored
Hardware:	The physical components which make up the computer (e.g. monitor, printer, drives etc.)
HTML	see **Hypertext Markup Language**
Hypertext Markup Language:	This is the programming language which allows you to create websites
Icon:	A small image which is used to represent a computer function or application
Information Society:	This is the name given to the society which is evolving from the change brought about by the impact of Information and Communication Technology
Information Superhighway:	This is a term used to convey the potential of the Internet to provide an easy but powerful way of communicating across the world
Input devices:	the hardware devices which allow you to enter data into the computer (e.g. keyboard, mouse etc.)
Integrated Service Digital Network (ISDN):	This is a high-speed, broadband link which is specially designed for digital data transmission
Internet Service Provider (ISP):	These are the organisations which provide you with access to the internet
Intelligent terminal:	This is a terminal or monitor which is linked to a personal computer so that locally it is linked to processing power
Internet:	This is the worldwide network of individual computers and computer networks which links millions of users
ISP	see **Internet Service Provider**
LAN:	see **Local Area Network**

Local Area Network:	A group of computers linked by cables so that they can communicate with each other in order to share resources, see also Integrated Service Digital Network and Wide Area Network
Mail merge:	This is a way of linking a wordprocessor to a file of information so that you can produce large numbers of customised letters or other documents
Mainframe Computer:	These are very large and powerful machines which require a team of specialist staff to operate and program them. They undertake large computational tasks such as keeping the accounts for an entire multinational company or government department
Memory:	Memory is the place where a computer works and stores information. Computers have several types of memory including Random Access Memory and Read Only Memory
Minicomputer:	Mini-computers were designed to provide medium-sized organisations or locations with computer power in cases where a main frame was too costly. They are far more robust than mainframes so they are used in industrial applications or in locations where mainframes would be uneconomical or impracticable. A single mini-computer and terminals form a computer network but mini-computers can be linked together to extend the network
Modem:	This is a device for linking computers together via a telephone line. The modem converts digital (computer) output into an analogue signal so that it can be sent down a telephone line. The signal is then converted back by a second modem so that the information can be understood by the second computer
Network computer:	This is a computer connected to many other computers
Object:	Within a Graphic User Interface most items which are displayed on the screen are known as objects
OCR	*see **Optical Character Reading***
Operating system:	The operating system is the software system (e.g. Microsoft Windows 98) which links the hardware and software together and provides many of the standard features of the computer. These include saving information on to the hard and floppy disks, printing documents, linking the keyboard and mouse to the application and presenting the information on the monitor
Optical Character Reading:	This is an application which works with a scanner to read written text into the computer
Output device:	These are the hardware devices which allow information to be outputted from the computer (e.g. monitor, printer etc.)
Personal Computer (PC):	A personal computer is essentially a machine designed for individual use. It consists of a monitor, system box, keyboard, mouse, various drives, CPU, motherboard and a variety of electronic cards
Peer-to-peer:	A limited form of computer network in which individual computers are linked directly together
Primary key:	This is a unique identifier of a database record (e.g. staff number and national insurance number)
PSDN	*see **Public Switched Data Network***
Public Switched Data Network:	The world telephone network is called the Public Switched Telephone Network
RAM	*see **Random Access Memory***

Random Access Memory (RAM):	This is working memory in which the computer carries out its functions once it is switched on. It only exists while the machine is on. If the power is switched off, so is the memory
Read Only Memory:	This is the permanent memory built into the computer through the silicon chips which make up the system
Refresh rates:	This is speed at which the screen is updated. The higher the rate the better the quality of the display
Resolution:	Digital pictures and displays are often described in terms of the numbers of pixels which make up the image (i.e.800 x 600). This is known as the resolution of the display or picture
ROM	see ***Read Only Memory***
RSI	see ***Repetitive Strain Injury***
Repetitive Strain Injury:	RSI is an injury brought about by carrying out an action in such a way that it places a strain on a person's body (e.g. arms, wrists and fingers). It can cause serious harm to you
Search Engine:	This is a software application which allows you to search for webpages containing particular information on the World Wide Web
Server:	A central computer which supports a network of the individual personal computers
Shortcut:	This is a way of initiating a command using a special combination of keys or by setting up an icon on the desktop
Software:	These are the electronic form of computer instructions and often takes the form of computer applications (e.g. wordprocessors, spreadsheets etc.)
URL:	URL (Uniform Resource Locator) is the unique address of a World Wide Web site that allows a browser to find a site
VDU	see ***visusal display unit***
Visual display unit:	This is another term for monitor
Virus:	Viruses are pieces of software which are designed to replicate themselves and to damage your computer system. They can delete your files, change your computer settings and fill up your storage with rubbish
WAN	see ***Wide Area Network***
Wide Area Network:	This is a network of computers over large geographical areas. A WAN can cover an individual town, county or even continent
Windows:	A window is a rectangular area of the screen in which computer applications and information is displayed
World Wide Web:	A large network of millions of websites spread across the world as part of the Internet
Zip drive:	This is a special device to backup computer information

Index